A.K. GANDHI

Published by

PRABHAT PRAKASHAN PVT. LTD.
4/19 Asaf Ali Road,
New Delhi-110 002 (INDIA)
e-mail: prabhatbooks@gmail.com

ISBN 978-93-5521-787-5
BARACK OBAMA: A COMPLETE BIOGRAPHY
by A.K. Gandhi

Edition
2025

Price
₹ 300 (Rupees Three Hundred Only)

Printed at
R-Tech Offset Printers, Delhi

Author's Note

What is most important thing in life that can lead you to success? I, as a writer and speaker, am often asked this question, and my response to this is simple, "Try gathering as much experience of practical life as may be possible". Barack Obama has fascinated me as a person because his decisions in office as the President were borne out of his wide and varied experience that he had chance to get in his life. A parallel to Obama's wide experience can be drawn with Narendra Modi who, riding on the ground experience in different places and posts, has gone on to scale the ladder of popularity in unprecedented terms. Now, the type of experience too counts much in shaping personality. In Obama's case, was the case of maturing, turning from indifference to active interest, from slackness to strength, from general to specific, from concrete to abstract; and together, all these went on to add charisma to his personality.

How I got more interested in Barack Obama was a quality of his school days which matches mine. Until high school, he was not really interested in reading, doing not so well in his academic grades; and then one day, beyond the expectations of all those who knew him then, he bought a box full of books rummaging from a roadside stall; and wonder, he read them all; but his vocabulary was yet small, so he understood little, but he did something that I too did in my school days right into the degree college. In his biography, A Promised Land, he writes: "Much of what I read I only dimly understood; I took to circling unfamiliar words to look up in the dictionary, although I was less scrupulous about decoding pronunciations—deep into my twenties I would know the meaning of words I couldn't pronounce". Something of the sort I did too. I used to write the words on the top or bottom margin of the page and went a step further as I also wrote the meaning on the side, so I wouldn't need to refer to the dictionary again, because I tended to forget words quite often, and I like to read books again and again. This has helped me build my vocabulary, as it did for Barack Obama.

Yet another aspect of Obama's personality: he is completely rooted in his family. He doesn't lose sight of his endearing wife and lovely daughters even when he is completely engaged with his professional work or writing, now or when he occupied the most powerful seat in the world. Whenever he has free time, he would prefer to pass it with his family, and also makes sure that he is in the company of his family members whenever and wherever he can. The period of presidentship was no different.

There are several other facets of Obama's personality that can endear him to any person. He never wondered if he would ever occupy the seat that is recognised as the most powerful one in the world, nor did anyone else, but he did with hard work and in style. Compare this exalted position with his humble backgrounds as he was born in Hawaii to a mother from Kansas and a father from Kenya, thus giving him African-American blood in his veins. He was raised with help from his grandparents, whose generosity of spirit reflected in his upbringing and the personality that he came to possess, and which ultimately enabled him to walk a challenging path to Presidentship of the US.

Ranked among the best presidents America has had, Obama continues to influence the world with his actions and words. His life presents us a view of the world that would make our thinking exalted; that makes reading his biography a must.

Contents

Author's Note 3

1. The Cultivation 9
2. Race to the Congress 28
3. Setting the Goal 37
4. The Race for Nomination 47
5. The Contest for Presidency 70
6. Taking on the World 89
7. Laurels and Later 140

The Cultivation

May 1, 2011, it was the day when the world that believes in humanity and peace erupted in a joyous roar after a brief amazement how it could have been accomplished, but it also brought gloom to a part of the world that believes in terrorism and unnecessary bloodbath; it was like a terrific shock to our neighbour, Pakistan. The occasion was that Osama Bin Laden had been eliminated in a way that was the most adequate way he should have been done away with, for he was the man behind the scores of innocent deaths over the world.

The celebration in the US was unprecedented, for the man behind the September 11 attacks had received the death he deserved best. Finally, the murderer of scores of people had been located and killed.

With the news, also broadcasted was a photograph of Barack Obama, the 44th President of the United States, sitting leisurely, in the Situation Room in the White House, with his curious eyes glued to the screen before him; on the screen was being relayed the live military action by the Navy SEALs that was undertaking the vital clandestine operation in the wee hours of the day in a friendly but treacherous country in Southeast Asia—Pakistan, where he was hiding in his Abbottabad compound.

Taking this type of decisions came natural to Obama; and we would need to explore his life right from childhood to understand how he came to inculcate this kind of aptitude.

Not coming from a political family, Obama was born on 4 August, 1961 at Honolulu in Hawaii. Located in the vast Pacific Ocean, this US state is not one of the 48 contiguous states; it is also the only US state outside the continent of North America and is located in the tropics; it was once an independent country that became a part of the US in 1959, and was the last state to be thus formed.

Obama's maternal grandparents came and settled in Hawaii in 1960, one year after it earned statehood. Separated from the rest of the US by a broad ocean, the atmosphere in the island state was quite different from what prevailed in the country, and was mostly apolitical.

Obama's mother, Ann Dunham was the only child of her parents with a lot of independent ideas and activities. She possessed political ideas too and often spoke about them, and her favourite topics included civil rights, Vietnam war, government corruption and women's movement. It was she that encouraged the then twelve-year-old Obama to watch the Watergate hearings every day, and she often sat close to him giving her views on the proceedings. To make easier for the readers, I would like to inform my readers that the Watergate was a political scandal that involved Richard Nixon, the US President, from 1972 to 1974, and finally led to his resignation. Under it, the Watergate Office Building in Washington was broken in to search the premises of the Democratic National Committee, and the Nixon administration took steps to cover up this attempt.

Ann Dunham taught the little Obama early moral lessons on how he should behave himself, and when she did, she spoke in no uncertain terms. Obama himself has acknowledged in his autobiography, *A Promised Land*, that she wanted him to grow up as a good citizen with positive values, but also gave him a chance to determine what was good and what was not. Once when he was reported to be part of a group in school that teased a kid, she peered into his eyes and asked what kind of person he would like to be: the one who doesn't care what happens to other people or the one who doesn't do things that hurt others. Obama feels that this question lingered in his mind for a long time, and guided him for several decisions in the times to come.

Obama portrays his mother as a lady, who had strong views and came bold on all issues, whether it suited one political block or the other. She was appalled by racism, and married outside her race not once but twice; and never shirked from her motherly duties for her two brown children: Obama and Maya.

Obama's father, Barack Obama Sr., was a married Luo Kenyan from Nyang'oma Kogelo. He married Ann Dunham in early 1961, a few months before Obama was born. The older Obama had been in the US on an educational scholarship to study undergraduate programme and then also did his postgraduation in economics at Harvard University. Their marriage did not last long, and they divorced in 1964. Obama Sr. visited his son at Hawaii only once in 1971. Recalling his father, Obama writes that it was the occasion when he saw him first and last; he only sent occasional letters which did not much motivate Obama. Obama Sr. died in a road accident in 1982; at this time, Obama was 21 years old.

Barack Obama has vividly described himself. Neither he, nor anybody else around ever imagined that he could be a budding leader in the times to come; rather he was viewed as a lackadaisical student, a passionate basketball player of limited talent and incessant, dedicated partyer. Politics was nowhere in the air; even in his peer groups, he never discussed politics. This disorderly youth was quite in contrast with the well-dressed, sharp person walking on the red carpet on more occasions than one as the President; the very imagination of being orderly would only qualify a pipedream even, so far-fetched the idea was; but then the world is a place where the most unexpected things takes place, and it did so for him. Not only did Obama become the President, he is also counted among the best ones that America has had.

Obama has a heart for his friends, and he not only remembers his friends from his early youth, but also has vivid memories about them, and the best part is that they are still in contact. He calls his company with friends as 'misspent youth'.

In youth, the question of racism had occurred to him on more occasions than one, and he had felt an underlying subtle discrimination against the blacks, in many avenues such as the society, game, films or school. He also realized that the scourge of racism did not limit to the phenomenon when the whites and the blacks came together, rather it even existed among people who were divided into segments on the basis of their social or financial status. He remembers his days in Indonesia where this kind of racism existed, and this gave him a feeling that the blacks and the whites were not unequal, they were only different and diverse. Thus, we see that his ideas had started to mature when he was still in early teens, and sometimes he was not sure what he should think of all these, as one kind of situation seemed to mingle and undercut others.

Maybe his mind was bogged down by such diversities that he best thought to find refuge in books, and her mother contributed in inculcating this habit. She would often tell him to go and read books, and the best part of this instruction was when she told him: "Then come back and tell me something you learned". This compelled the young Obama to read rather carefully.

Obama spent part of his youth in Hawaii when his mother was away in Indonesia and it was there that she raised Maya; and this period was like a lull in his life because he did not learn as much as he was supposed to because his mother was not around him. When he was in tenth grade, his grandparents took him to a rummage sale, where he was attracted to fat hardcover books and he pulled out several titles including those of Ralph Ellison and Langston Hughes, Robert Penn Warren and Dostoyevsky, DH Lawrence and Ralph Waldo Emerson. Those around him never believed their eyes because Obama was never found immersed in books. But this time, he proved them wrong as he not only read them, but also acquired more.

However, it was like the first free confrontation with the books, and he was yet to learn much to know the meanings and pronunciations of all the words that he found in the books; and to overcome at least the obstacle of the meanings. He started to circle the words and look for their meanings in the dictionary. This enlarged his vocabulary, but it had a large number of words whose meanings he was sure about but did not know how to pronounce correctly.

It was his interest in books that probably assisted in his admission to the Occidental College in 1979; yet Obama felt about himself that he had half-cooked knowledge of the current issues. The college brought him to a platform with varied experiences in diverse ideologies of socialism to capitalism. As he thought himself inadequate to mix up with the advanced lot, he befriended those from the lower strata of students, and also those from other cultures like Pakistan or India; this gave him a clear idea how the world operates because these students came from communities that have suffered over the decades and centuries and have faced actual struggles. An economic policy that would mean little for a well-to-do student could be a life-devastating or life-building one for the one who belonged to these communities; and this was here that he developed sympathies with them. This was how his two years' stay at this college led to his political awakening, admits Obama. His political awakening was more to do with social movements involving ordinary people.

As his realization of the community problems expanded, he became alive to the problems that confronted the workers and those demanded political rights, including those in India and South Africa, and this was how he started to take inspiration from the likes of Gandhiji, Nelson Mandela, Lech Walesa and Dr. King, among others. He had also started to realize his mother's words that real power lay, not in suppressing and crushing the suppressed people, but lifting them up. He was becoming aware of the functional democracy in true sense of the word, in which the depressed classes did not get their rights as a gift from those in the high strata, but they earned it through the functioning of democracy maintaining their dignity and unity.

The next three years after the Occidental College at Columbia University led to the real realization as he spent most time in reading and writing, and mostly stayed away from college parties or mess debates. The more he read, the more questions lingered in his mind, and to quench his thirst for answering such questions, he further probed the literature he could lay his hands upon, and the university library came handy in this endeavour. It was the era when some very original questions cropped up in his mind, and he was becoming very interested to find answers to them. The questions ranged from asking himself why some movements fail while others succeed, when a compromise was the best solution and when it was not so, and how one can know the difference between the two. This period can be called the true one in which he grew up mentally, forming up his ideas; these ideas were going to provide him the foundation on which he would be able to take crucial decisions at the helm.

Obama had been brought up in a Hawaiian and Indonesian setting, so he was a bit shy by nature with a deep sense of self-consciousness but wrapped in fundamental laziness. He decided to overcome this shortcoming with a practical outlook. He also tried to overcome his softness, but he admits that he could not do this to his own satisfaction. In his deep soul, he felt that he needed to prepare himself for a greater contest in the world, yet he was not sure what it was. He had learned from his family not to have staunch ideas, yet stand as a proud American who took pride in his nationhood, in celebrating his religious celebrations and national festivals, yet he never wore these spirits on his sleeves. Their patriotism was something lying deep in their psyche which they thought unnecessary to put on their foreheads just to show it off.

The idea of America was simply the respect for rights of everybody that was devoid of any kind of discrimination on grounds of race, religion or any other factor. He believed that all men are created equal, and this spirit made up his America. He also realized that no nation, or even man could be perfect in ideology and practice, so was America and he himself; but that never meant that an effort should not be made for improvement, that's what he felt deep inside him.

Obama graduated in 1983; and he had great ideas in his mind, yet he could find no leader around him from whom he could derive inspiration. He decided to work at the grassroots level, and this brought him to Chicago. It is the same city where way back in 1893 Swami Vivekananda had delivered his popular speech in the Parliament of the World's Religions as a representative of Hinduism, and took the world by storm when he began his speech by saying: "Sisters and brothers of America...". Until now, Hinduism was considered a backward, pagan religion.

Arrival in Chicago brought Obama to work with churches that were working to stabilise communities which had suffered owing to the closures of steel plants. At this time, he had joined as the director of the 'Developing Communities Project', a church-based community organisation, comprising eight parishes in southern Chicago. He worked on it until 1988. At this time, he also worked as a consultant and instructor for the Gamaliel Foundation, a community organising institute.

As he organised movements, he came closer to the common people, and this also brought changes in the lower communities. This work brought much change in him. He was once again feeling confident, which was evident with a perennial smile playing up his lips. This also gave him an idea that people together mattered because their combined voices mattered. In this progress, he found that the values he learnt from his mother and grandparents were very useful. These were the values of honesty, hard work and empathy; these could function as a common thread between people, helping them to come together.

While he was still busy in organising people, he felt that his work achieved not much and it was taking more time than it should, so he would have to think more broadly. However, he had seen the power of people coming together as he saw that the movement in Chicago resulted in the election of a Black mayor. He was now gradually evolving ideas that could lift him from the grassroots campaigning to wider perspectives, without losing sight of the importance of the power that lay at the layman's level, because only that could fetch votes needed to bring about a substantial change.

The election of a Black man gave hopes to Obama that he too could run for a public office one day; of course, election to be the President was too farfetched even at this stage. At the same time, he was well aware of the pitfalls of running for a public office, as it could involve constant struggle for power, making compromises, which could not be accomplished without chasing money and sometimes abandoning the very ideals that one stood for, and you could not make an impression without power in your hand. This all made things quite messy.

He was yet undecided how he should go about it in order to bring about a change in the institutions that could result into a wider change in the country. It was at this time one Christmas, that his mother advised him to seek that change in the institutions from inside. She gave her example that she had worked with various movements from outside, but she could not contribute in realizing her ideology. Studying law further gave impetus to what he thought of movements and politics and what the government should do in relation to the society, market and other factors of national life. Media attraction won him a contract to write a book on racial relations; though this book evolved into memoirs titled Dreams from My Father.

Obama enrolled at the Harvard Law School in 1988. It was during his law studies that he was elected as the first Black head of the Law Review, which generated media interest. It was at this stage that he signed a contract to write a book. Job offers came which could lead him to try his hand at politics someday. He could have worked for a fat salary for a law job, but then he decided otherwise. He indeed clerked for a law firm at Harvard.

In 1991, Obama accepted a two-year position as Visiting Law and Government Fellow at the University of Chicago Law School. He taught constitutional law for twelve years, first as a lecturer and then as a senior lecturer. During this stint, he continued to organise community movements, and in the Project Vote, he led the registration of 150,000 voters out of a total of 400,000 unregistered African-Americans at that time. This work earned him the title "40 Under 40 Powers to Be" by Crain's Chicago Business in 1993.

In 1993, Obama joined the law firm "Davis, Miner, Barnhill & Galland" and fought cases involving civil rights litigation and neighbourhood economic development, first as an associate and then as an attorney. As a lawyer, he also took part in a number of well publicised cases which involved important organisations including the Citibank.

It was at this stage that Obama met Michelle who came to Harvard as part of the Sidley recruiting team, and they did not take long to have shared sentiments about many facets of life, which led to a mutual love between them. Time passed quicker than he thought, and soon it was time for him to go back to Chicago, which he informed Michelle unfolding what he had in his mind about his future. It was at this time that he had been looking for avenues to work for a public office if possible. Michelle supported him and advised that he should go for what he felt right. As their ideas blended, they married after several years of dating, on 3 October, 1992. They were destined to have a shared future now. They led an ordinary life, working and enjoying together. That went on until 1995 until a political opportunity knocked at their doors.

This political opportunity was not the one which he could have wished. It came when the sitting Congressman from the Second District of Illinois had been indicted on several legal charges which could deprive him his seat in the Congress. To replace him, the local state senator threw her hat in; and it was to fight election for this state senate seat that Obama was supposed to contest for the remaining term. He himself did not want to go for this as the state capital, Springfield was not to his taste, and Michelle too did not want to go there. When she finally consented that he could contest for this seat, she put in a condition that she would not be asked to live in Springfield anytime.

Obama sought the consent of his mother who was suffering from uterine cancer recuperating in Hawaii then, yet she was in high spirits as usual. His sister Maya too encouraged him to go for this, and this was how Obama set off on his maiden political campaign. The campaign was as simple as it could be. There were no media, no researchers, no TV or radio guys; the audience were served simple chips and drinks, and the supporters were never more than a few hundred. The only campaign placard was only eight-by-four-inch card with a passport photograph and a few bulleted information which he himself had tapped on his computer. He sought some professional help, after all, contesting an election is a serious matter and has to be undertaken earnestly.

Obama recalls the campaign days and how it worked to groom him as a politician. Earlier, he had undertaken campaigns while remaining in the background, but now he was supposed to be a frontrunner. Earlier, he was a humorous and inspired spirit, but being in the forefront, he could not be in his natural self, and was described to be serious and dumb. Still, the voters could see in him a serious contestant, and this helped to bring in more supporters. As the people around him gathered in greater numbers, he became more accustomed, more relaxed and more spontaneous. This was how he came in the limelight.

His campaign had barely started when it hit upon a roadblock. The previous state senator, Alice Palmer was supposed to vacate the state seat after she got elected for the Congress, but she lost the election. She had earlier promised Obama that she would not be running for the state senate whatever the outcome. Politicians are poorly known for keeping their word, so it was a matter of worry for Obama. The worst fears came true. Politics is rightly called the dirty game, a game of power at whatever cost. She intended to go for the senate seat.

Obama felt somewhat confident because he had been campaigning for this senate seat for the past few months and had won the endorsements of a few elected officials; but Alice Palmer running for the seat could put the matter upside down as she commanded sizeable support. Obama thought over his chances, and then decided to go for it. He filed his papers with the Chicago Board of Election Commissioners and he won the ruling. Alice dropped out. The hardest battle was over. There was no Democrat opponent in his way, and the Republican opposition was hardly any matter.

Obama made it to the state senate but not without learning the vital lessons of politics, and how winning was different from losing, what kind of hard words politics requires, and despite your wish to be fair, politics has little room for being fair.

Obama's mother died of uterine cancer in Hawaii in 1995. He was heartbroken and all his memories with her came rushing by in a large panorama of thoughts. He earnestly completed all the required rites before returning to his job as the senator.

Obama needed to visit Springfield on and off, and he drove himself for three hours and a half; and this time gave him time to tune to audiobooks—novels and history books. This gave him an opening into the inner politics and he availed this opportunity to form connections beginning with assisting other senators in their campaigns and coming closer to them in games of golf and basketball and over drinks. This also gave him an opportunity to serve the cause of the blacks. He also learnt a lesson or two in how to go about law-making, and also how to not allow the state funds to go for personal luxuries of the leaders and those who mattered. His education in law helped him put his statements and arguments forcefully winning applaud. Working for the poor is not always easy for a politician because their interests often conflict with those of the rich; and it could deprive him of the financial support that comes from the industry and the powers-that-be, though few would acknowledge it.

Obama thought about this factor as it could prove to be a roadblock for his progress in politics. He realized that getting support from actual supporters is what matters most, and to his dismay, he found that his work in the senate was not attracting many voters. They were almost indifferent to what was going on in the senate. To overcome this, he decided to come closer to his voters, and for this, he started writing a regular column for the Hyde Park Herald, a small weekly with a readership of few thousand people. It was a small effort. He tried other ways too to attract attention, but not with much success. He realized that all this was leading to a futile effort because his party was in a miniscule minority in the senate.

Michelle suffered a miscarriage and the couple decided to go for in vitro fertilisation for conception. They had their first daughter, Malia Ann in 1998, and the second daughter, Sasha in 2001. Obama is very close to his daughters and often finds time for his family. He has often described his daughters and family in his books, and shows how close he is to them and how intensely he feels for them. He is psychologically with them even when he is physically apart. His writings about his family are worth reading for any person who has or wishes to have a happy family. Obama loves dogs too. His invitations bear the dogs' names too, that shows the animal lover in him. The books he wrote started to get attention in the market and contributed to a sizeable part of his earnings. With rise of his popularity, this income was going to increase manifolds. In 2010, Michelle claimed that Obama had quit smoking.

Obama is a Protestant Christian. He has written that he was not born in a religious family. He has described his mother as the one 'detached from religion' but 'spiritually awakened in many ways', and praises her for her secular humanism. He acknowledges his biological father as a 'confirmed atheist', and he found his stepfather who found 'religion as not particularly useful'. In contrast to his parents, Obama cultivated religious beliefs in his adulthood when he worked with Black churches in his twenties, and he came to understand how the African-American religious tradition has the potential to bring about social change to the common masses. In 2008, Obama stated that he is a devout Christian, and believes in the redemptive death and resurrection of Jesus Christ. He also believes that religion has shown him a path to be cleansed of sin and have an eternal life. He has asserted his religious beliefs on more occasions than one. In 2010, he acknowledged that he did not come from a religious family, yet cultivated his religious beliefs and iit was because the precepts of Jesus Christ spoke to me in terms of the kind of life that I would want to lead'. He claims to have learnt from religion how to support his kith and kin and 'how to treat others as they would treat me.

Despite his admission to the importance of religion in his life, Obama does not bear it on his sleeves. He and his family members do not attend church on a regular basis.

The American society is an open one, in which man and wife contribute to housework almost on an equal basis, as both of them have a career to look after. Obama too wanted to do his share, but he admits that he was not able to do much because 'he was trying to deliver a lot of things to a lot of different people', and this caused a little argument between them as the little children required constant tending, and Michelle wanted him to share homely duties. He realized his duty to his daughters, and this brought him closer to them. He finds time to talk to them even during his busy schedule; a father's heart beats inside him, all the time.

❑❑

Race to the Congress

Michelle was reluctant to stay in Springfield and she often questioned if her husband's hard work in the Senate was worth the outcome; she wanted him to concentrate on his profession. Instead Obama decided to run for the Congress. While she wanted him to relieve him of the load, he had decided to carry a heavier load on his head; he wanted a more influential office for himself. He thought that Michelle would be better off in Washington instead of being in Springfield, and so he announced his candidacy for the Congress from the First Congressional District.

Politics is a dirty game, an unpredictable one, and it's all the same the world over, in the US too; and the issues raised in elections are not different either: Obama is an outsider, he is backed by white folks, he is a Harvard elitist; he is Black! And so forth.

The race was not going to be an easy one, as there are many things involved than one can think of, and one has to pay attention to them, as they can make or mar the final outcome. Riding on the wave of sympathy, Obama's competitor won. Obama wondered if he had taken a wrong turn and if he had become a bad politician. Being busy with the election and the related activities, he could give little time to his family, leading to a strained marriage.

Seeing all negative things happening around, Obama decided to wait and allow good times to come on, and he continued to first mope and then work to bring things round his point. At the same time, he gave time to his family. It was during this time that on 10 June, 2001, his second daughter Sasha was born, giving him a 'blast of joy'. The foursome together spent quality time for a couple of years. This lull brought him peace, it was a kind of letting go of his passions and desires, bringing out the best of a father and a husband in him. All this while, his political career was on a lower side. Of course, he used this time to construct ties with the common people in different parts of the constituency for which he wanted to contest election for the Congress. Even at this stage, his ambition was not far-fetched, he just wanted to win the election, and quit politics on a high, he felt.

During his interactions with common people, he realized that national politics could not change so long as people remained indifferent and unknown to all others around; and this would continue to be exploited by politicians to feed the stereotypes like pitting the Blacks against the Whites or natives against the immigrants, or the rural people against the urban ones. If such an ideal situation were created, even the staunchest politician would have to pay heed to the common interests of all people, rather than serving and appeasing the vote-banks, as is called in our India. Obama felt that such a situation would even compel the media to take notice of the people as a whole, and then bring out stories hinging on common good, rather than on focussing on the divides and differences to bring the negative out. In other words, he wanted to build a bridge across the country's racial, ethnic and religious divides. He felt that it could be a high call, but he wanted to work in this direction.

Despite his wish to start bridge-building politics, Obama was also aware that it could not suit to the race for the Congress. This also meant assuaging the wounds of the Blacks who have often felt being discriminated against by the Whites, and they often asked him how well he could stand up against those who have taken advantage of them and those who look down on them. He decided that he would have to speak for the widest possible audience, and bring relief to them on two counts; one was to bring big projects to solve the developmental shortcomings, and the second was to address the people's plight in personal field, such as healthcare, education and employment. Politics could be much more than what people think it merely is. With this kind of thinking, he now earnestly wanted to contest for a seat in the US Senate.

Obama was now mentally ready to go for the election, but he had to face an obstacle on the home front. At this time, Michelle was working as the executive director for community affairs at the University of Chicago hospital system, and had to pay a lot of attention to her job and career. He thought that she might not consent to his entering the poll politics, but when he approached her, she wanted to discuss it, but in the company of some people so that she could get the right advice.

Obama, Michelle and four others gathered over a lengthy brunch. Obama presented his case, explaining what he thought all about this, how he could win the nomination, and how his race to the Senate was to be different from the last one; and concluded his case with a simple statement that he would be done with politics if he lost this race.

Michelle was convinced but was hindered on the finances. The last election had drained on the family savings, and the family had yet to respond properly to their debts and credit card advances and had to save enough for the daughters' education, and Obama would not be able to practise law, meaning that they would be hard on finances; in addition, they would have to manage money for the new election. The two scenarios were quite hopeless: she felt if he lost, they would be in a financial mess, and if he won, they would have to maintain two households in Washington and Chicago, meaning they would be under financial pressure. The situation was literally 'out of the frying pan and straight into the fire'.

Obama took a deep sigh and then countered this thinking saying that he would be able to draw national recognition, and if he lost, it would help him get an offer to write another book that would sell a lot of copies, and winning would mean having a higher profile as he would be the only African-American in the Senate.

Michelle was hanging balance between the uncertainties and her husband's ambitions. She consented to his taking part in the election, but not before comparing the entire situation to having a few magical beans in his pocket which he would plant, which would become a giant beanstalk overnight, and he would climb up it, kill the giant and bring home a goose that laid golden eggs. She okayed, but said that she would not take part in the campaigning.

Learning from the failures of the previous election, Obama was now mentally ready to take on the challenge for the US Senate seat. He decided where he needed to put emphasis for his campaign. It was to focus more on one-to-one connections than policy matters, on media connections, and on putting up his ideas on how to go about different bills, so that people knew what stand he was likely to take in case he was elected. He also expressed his views on a slew of issues and matters that he would like to pay attention to; he was doing all this to strengthen his case as an effective legislator and also as a thinker.

Building up his image in this manner helped him; and some other factors also went in his favour. Two of the contestants who could have run for the Democrat seat had decided not to contest. This helped him as the media went after him seeking his views on crucial matters, including the invasion of Iraq. Issues like this had to be tackled tactfully, because after 9/11, a majority of people were in the favour of the war, and going against the wishes of people could ruin the chances of his candidacy. Taking part in a rally, which was dubbed as anti-war rally, Obama as the main speaker went on to state that he stood before the people as someone who was not opposed to war in all circumstances, rather he said he was opposed to dumb wars. He then made out his case that there was no need to invade Iraq since Saddam Hussein posed no imminent threat to the country. He then also went on to explain the uncertainty that America was supposed to confront there. He finally recommended that the country should first work against al-Qaeda, stop supporting repressive regimes and be not dependent on oil from the Middle East.

It was a new stance; and people cheered in the rally; though the media did not take much note of this stand. Not many days had passed when the US-led coalition began bombing Baghdad, and the casualties and other losses soon made Democrats turn against the Iraq War. With this, the press too turned against this operation asking questions that should have been asked before all this mess was started. And surprisingly, all that Obama had said at the rally became relevant all of a sudden. This made him a prominent leader who spoke logical things. People started donating to him and his cause of contesting the election was never stronger before.

Obama was now more earnest in his approach, building person-to-person contacts in ethnic communities and food joints, where he could speak to people. His visits to the suburban areas mounted. He spoke on the issues that concerned common people, like ending tax breaks for companies outsourcing jobs or promoting renewable energy or helping the cause of higher education for the poor children. At the centre of his talks was of course the Iraq war asking why the brave soldiers were being made to sacrifice themselves only for the sake of a war, as it was yet far from over with Osama bin Laden still out of sight.

Obama not only spoke, but also listened; and the more he listened, the more people were wont to speak up their minds, and this gave him an idea what people wanted, and he could mould his election campaign accordingly.

One thing he had understood very clearly, that was about health insurance.

Soon, Obama was becoming popular because he spoke what people wanted him to speak; he spoke for them. He promised that he would make the government make a slight change in policies that would help people live a better life.

By the beginning of 2004, Obama had created a favourable air for himself in Chicago. He also issued two ads just four weeks prior to the primaries; one of them had the tagline "Yes we can", and the other showed the statement by Sheila Simon, the daughter of the state's former senator Paul Simon who had died just before he planned to endorse Obama as the next candidate. More support followed as more newspapers supported and endorsed him. This benefited him greatly as Obama won the primaries with a considerable margin. He had his own way of thanking people for the support; he went down to the Central Station to shake hands with commuters; and as people recognised him, more and more people poured to shake hands and share a smile. The next goal did not seem far off.

The main election was yet a few months away, but the campaign built up gradually. The comfortable margin that he had secured went on to make him a popular figure as he won a sizeable air time on the media. The most amazing thing was that people of all segments liked to listen to what he wanted to say; and he was saying all that people would want to listen. The battle was not going to be easy, because his opponent, the Republican Jack Ryan too had been working for poor people, especially for the disadvantaged kids.

Electioneering can sometimes be very dirty, as the opponent employed people tail Obama almost everywhere so as to catch him in a gaffe. But the outcome was just like God's revenge. The final blow to Jack Ryan came when the press published the sealed records from Ryan's divorce in which his ex-wife had alleged that he had pressured her to visit sex clubs and had tried to coerce her into having sex in front of strangers. Nothing could go worse than this for a candidate. He had no other way but to withdraw from the race.

And for good, Obama had no opponent now. Despite being sure to enter the Senate, Obama did not lower his guard. He continued to gruel himself in the campaign. He wanted to leave nothing to chance. His work fascinated people, and he became a popular figure. Wherever he went, people followed him; even children were not far behind. Many of them would come and say, “I saw you on TV. Aren’t you the same?” Michelle's magic beans story seemed to materialise for now.

Obama was sworn in on 3 January, 2005 as the US Senator from Illinois.

❑❑

Setting the Goal

When Obama had started his election campaign two years ago, he had told his wife that rising to the post of a Senator would be the high position he would be contented with; but now it was no more the case. From the very moment he took the oath of office, he had his eyes on presidency. And the situation was quite favourable to him too. Ordinarily, senators struggle to get the media attention, but here the case was quite the opposite; the media was after him to seek his views on almost every matter that needed the national attention. Not only this, the reporters went after him asking him to reveal his plans, and he was surprised when he was asked if he wished to go for the presidency. He often wondered if he should go for governorship and not presidency, because he was yet very young, just forty-three at this time. He also realized that he could pace down a bit because he had just started out on the national scene, and had much time to go for these coveted posts. He says: "I figured I had all the time in the world".

Right from the outset in the Congress, Obama wanted to carve his path to the highest post in the country by taking inspiration from what Hillary Clinton had done. She worked diligently and made it perceptible; she worked with substance through her work, and she paid attention to the constituency, so that she could remain in their current memory. Obama too decided to be a 'workhorse' and not a 'show horse', as he termed it.

Obama set his office in order, and then went on to study the issues that he could raise, the bills he could propose and the senators who could be advantageous to him in his strategy. He had to fight another inclination; the senior senators never wanted a junior senator to hog more limelight than they could. He was starting to learn how to survive and also do better. He learnt that you should be capable enough to take the punches, and never give up. Fighting the odds is another name for survival in the cutthroat business of politics.

Obama had a penchant for being in close contact with people, and as a senator, he made efforts to further add vigour to this effort, and for this, he opened a number of offices to remain in touch with the public. These offices included those located Chicago, Washington and several other small towns. He deputed professional people to head these offices, and clearly instructed that people might or might not like the way he voted in the Senate, but no email should go unanswered. He had clearly instructed his offices that any important matter should be brought to his notice immediately.

In his first year in the Senate, Obama felt like a reprise of his early years in the Illinois legislature, but now the stakes were higher. Like he was always wont to, he continued to observe things that unfolded around him; how people wrapped their interests in the garb of grand principles; he also noticed that the senators were in general well informed of different current topics. He also saw that the senate committees often dragged on with discussions, often pointless, only adding to the grievances of the affected ones; he also saw how members consumed hundred words to say what they could well have said in less than ten. He also noticed, and not too happily, that often the discussions took the line to undermine the party and senators in opposition rather than serving the need of the people and the nation.

Despite being in the limelight at the national level, he did not lose sight of his family. He often travelled to Chicago to pass quality time with the family. Whenever he was home, he would ensure that he wasn't too busy, he took time out to read a book to Malia at bedtime or shuttling Sasha to the dance class. He maintained good relations with his servants and driver, and they were like his family members. On the finances front also, things improved as he bought a new house in Kenwood. Better finances allowed Obama to request his mother-in-law, Marian to reduce her working hours and help look after the young girls. And the fun of having her in the house was great as she defended him whenever he was late to return home or when things otherwise went messy on the domestic front. This only helped better the relationship between man and wife, as they had not been able to spend much time together. The couple often decided to stay away from the limelight so that they could pass their evenings with the daughters.

The couple liked to socialise and also attend dinners, but then the things were not as simple as they were earlier, because they could easily be identified in the crowd, and people often scurried to take photographs with them. People often tried to strike long conversations with them, or when they went for dinner in restaurants, those on the nearby tables went silent, only in an effort to overhear what they were talking about.

An important access that Obama got as a senator was to have a say in foreign affairs, and this opening would give him a chance to be a more mature politician who could polish his views about the problems facing the world in which American interests were involved. The first foreign visit for him in this capacity was to Russia because the abandoned nuclear establishments in the former Soviet Russia were under a terrorist threat, and they needed to be guarded from falling into vicious hands. It was a great visit learning about the finer nuances of foreign affairs.

This one was the first, but certainly not the last in this capacity, as he went on to visit a number of countries as part of delegations; and these countries included England, Mexico and several others. He was pained to see the destruction that the war had brought upon Iraq and its people. He found that the actions of his government were wrong when its forces moved into Iraq bringing misery everywhere. In his memoirs he writes that he, "Couldn't shake the thought of those kids paying the price for the arrogance" of the American government, though initiated by a few people supporting the war. He did not limit himself in seeing the terrible situation in other countries, but also thought how he could help people out there.

A great personality feature of Obama is that he is greatly moved by the people's plight occurring due to any reason, including natural calamities, accidents or poor government policies. He tried to assuage the wounds through his visits and do whatever could be possible in his capacity as the senator; and he often approached government officials and secretaries to bring to their attention the dire needs that should be fulfilled by the government. He was very particular and found himself among the TV debates arguing for people's welfare. He brought out the fact that forgotten people and forgotten voices existed all over the country, and he insisted that America as a whole should invest in tackling the isolation, intergenerational poverty and lack of opportunities that persisted in large areas of the country. In this way, he was making an effort to serve the needs of not only his constituency, but also others where racism had brought development below par. He possessed a holistic view about problems whether they were environmental, financial, employment, societal or others.

His acumen and vigour, his thought process and positive inclination, his contact with people and empathy all led people to believe that he would be the fittest candidate for presidency, and when people met him, they did not shy away from expressing their views, and it only strengthened Obama's trust in himself that he could well go for the high post. The momentum gradually built up and by the spring of 2006, he started to feel that presidency was no longer outside the realm of possibility. Of course, in the beginning, he did not want speculations to go wild on the media, so he was wont to give 'rote denials' for any such attempt. However, he was now making earnest efforts in this direction, which involved meeting Democratic candidates in the midterms, holding meetings with influential party officials and accessing donors.

This approach led him to confront new audiences, and he started to build a ground for himself, though he continued to demur. All this while, he wondered if he was fooling himself or others about his candidacy.

He continued to travel across the country building his support and contacts. He had correctly understood that running for the high post needed a consistent long-term effort with confidence and conviction; but he also realized that running for presidency required piles of money and enough commitment and goodwill. After all, winning from a couple of states could not lead to success; he would have to become an acceptable name in most of, if not all, states.

Running for presidency for Obama was not going to be easy either; because there were others who had been preparing for this for years, including Joe Biden who ultimately came to power in 2021 defeating Trump. All these people had built up a momentum in their support through a dedicated staff, donors and officials, and who had much to show in achievements like meaningful legislative measures. In contrast, Obama could not boast of such high accomplishments, though he had started to appear as a favourite figure for presidency.

Obama also knew that the positive favour he had gained in the media could not be fully trusted because it could become adverse at any moment if any other candidate appeared stronger than him. He deeply considered what all he would need before he could present himself as a serious contender, and this could include several aspects in policy initiatives as well as language and attitude that he would have to adopt to become a favourite with the people.

Obama was yet unsure if he should acquire more experience as a senator before running for presidency, when his doubts were alleviated by people who said that his strength lay in the fact that he could motivate people, especially young people, minorities, even middle-of-the-road people; and moreover, they felt that ten more years in the Senate would not make him a better president. Many people also recommended that common people wanted something different, and he could satisfy these demands. Even his co-politicians in the party now had started to support the idea that he should positively think about going for election. What he was inspired by was the words that a senior senator, Teddy Kennedy said to him. He said that the moments like that are rare. He said that he might think he was not ready and that he would do it at a more convenient time but "You don't choose the time; the time chooses you". It was a great inspiration; the message is for all people to take cognisance of: Either you seize what may turn out to be the only chance you have, or you decide you are willing to live with the knowledge that the chance has passed you by.

The toughest obstacle that Obama felt lay in the way of deciding if he should go for presidency was none other than his sweetheart wife, Michelle. She had reluctantly agreed when he went for the state elections, and then for the Senate; and now he wanted her consent to run for presidency. She was reluctant to consent. Obama felt that circumstances might have opened the door to a presidential race, but nothing could prevent him from closing it, though it was becoming harder by the day to do so. As the time passed, people stressed upon him to reveal his plan for presidency, but he could not afford to do so because family life for him was equally important.

In fact, Michelle disliked how their family life had been invaded by the public eye and they were not able to lead a normal life as citizens. She was also aware that the process of running for the presidency could be exhilarating, but it would be mostly misery; it would be like a continuous stress test—how much they could bear. In fact, the whole thing could turn out to be so crazy, undignified and brutal.

By December 2006, the time had come when the final decision had to be made whether Obama should go for the highest post in the land, and the occasion was a meeting in Hawaii. It was at this meeting that Michelle asked him boldly why he needed to be president, and how he could be different from other Democrats in that capacity.

Obama stared at her across the table. All these thoughts rose in a tempest; he wanted to say many things, that it would be like a family pride, or that he would serve the people like no other president had done; he could well have said so many things, but then he checked his emotions and said what set the mood of his better half in a positive realm. He started saying that he could say that he might be able to spark a new kind of politics, or get a new generation to participate, or bridge the divisions in the country better than other candidates could; but then he added that he could give no guarantee to that; but one thing he knew for sure, and he said: "I know that the day I raise my right hand and take the oath to be president of the United States, the world will start looking at America differently. I know that kids all around this country - Black kids, Hispanic kids, kids who don't fit in - they'll see themselves differently, too, their horizons lifted, their possibilities expanded. And that alone...that would be worth it".

With these words, the entire hall sank in a deep thought. He could hear in this 'deafening' silence Michelle saying that it was a really good answer. Finally, the last obstacle had been crossed safely, but the fight that lay ahead was yet to be started in right earnest.

❑❑

The Race for Nomination

It was in February 2007 that Obama announced in Springfield that he was now a candidate for president. The morning was bright and cold, and a new aura seemed to have been added to it with this announcement. When he had planned this occasion, he was scared that there would be only a few people to attend this; but he was overjoyed to see that a strong crowd of about fifteen thousand people waited to hear the announcement. This declared how people were crazy about his presidency. What gave the occasion a festive mood was the fact that people wore OBAMA signs that had been provided at the venue.

Enthused with the response, Obama outlined what his campaign would be like and what the issue he was going to raise in the days to come. He insisted on a fundamental change that needed to be brought about in the administration and governance; and assured people to tackle long-term problems like healthcare and climate change. He assured that the days of Washington partisan divide were numbered and the time had come to move past the parochial attitude.

Everything unfolded on a positive note. The media coverage was broad and positive; everything seemed to fall in its place. The media chased him all over, people described this as ‘not normal’. It was like a magical ride that could catch lightning in a bottle and tap into something that would display the undaunted American spirit. While for most candidates, the beginning is made from small meetings and local networks, but in case of Obama, everything seemed to be magnificent; wherever he went, a feeling like that of the Times Square came.

The media glare right from the day one could also lead to negative flashes, as Obama was yet inexperienced when it came to it compared with other candidates. He had to guard himself against 'gaffes' that candidates are often wont to express. These only reveal their ignorance, carelessness, insensitivity or unclear thinking. His team warned him not to commit any such foolery, because the media could easily blow it out of proportions and that could destroy his campaign from the very outset. ‘Think thrice before you speak’ was the warning that his team gave him with the clear instruction that this had to be followed whether the media was around or not, because you can never believe who was doing what in this modern age when digital tools were available in every pocket and virtually anybody could be capable of making something viral on the social media. He faced this situation early in his campaign when he said that "three thousand of our young troops' lives had been wasted in Iraq", but fortunately, this gaffe was not well picked by the media.

Obama faced a problem in his early campaign speeches because he was inclined to analyse the issues in great details, rather than favouring or disfavouring them. He often classified the problem into more categories than simple positive or negative, and this posed him a problem when he had to take a decision. He was warned that he need not cut open any issue in so many parts where one part could stand in opposition to another. So, brevity was an important virtue that he had to observe in his speeches, he learnt.

Whenever Obama was not in Washington in connection with the Senate business, he would be in Iowa or some other state for a long day out, meeting people, visiting cafes, holding meetings, giving interviews, contacting donors, shaping his campaign, listening to people, planning for the next day campaign; all this was like a grind because he worked almost sixteen hours a day, six days and a half a week. All this time he slept barely for five or six hours and tried to compress as many activities as he could, barely finding time to contact back home to be in touch with his lovely daughters. Busy to the last strand of hair, he did not miss his daily workout, locating treadmills wherever he went, and often, he found himself in a funny situation. Such a grinding routine was to continue not for a week or two, but for the coming one year and a half; he describes this as "not glamour but monotony", and such a tiring schedule could wear down his spirit.

In his campaign for presidency, Obama found it toughest to command a big team who did a variety of tasks for him, to beg strangers for money, and propagate a vision that he believed in. All this while, what he missed was rest, a quality time with his family, and of course, sitting at a proper table for a proper meal. All this while, he needed to keep in touch with the current affairs, what was going on around him, and what his opponents were doing in their campaigns. He had to learn the fine points of issues like child welfare and education, new technology and how America should interact with different countries, and what stand it should take on different issues confronting the world.

Obama realized that he had to learn the essence of different issues with quite a difficulty, and he had to master the way he could convey to people all these issues in a story-like finesse which could touch their hearts creating a favourable environment for him. While he had to understand issues in his favour, he had also to find the counter points to the issues that his opponents were raising, because it is the perspective that a candidate presents to his audiences to earn people's appreciation.

Obama had also to overcome his approach while dealing with people. When people put up questions to him, he tried to answer them; but then he was advised by his team to not merely answer questions but also pass his message across, and not limit himself to answering questions. They also briefed him how he could bypass questions while putting across his message; because the questions could at times be misleading and they could trip him up. They could well be a trap, and he had to avoid them, overcome them and still be able to present his views without getting downplayed. The important points for a politician were not answering questions, but to evoke an emotion, or identify an enemy, or signal to a constituency that he would favour. He had to change his approach because he found that people were impressed not with facts but with emotions.

All this while, his team was doing well, helping to keep him motivated and sharing the burden of his work, yet he could not afford to lower his guard. His team comprised Gibbs, Marvin Nicholson and Reggie Love among many others, who looked after what Obama could need in diverse situations. There were people in his team who were stationed at different places to serve his goal, though they were seldom seen in public. Even he himself was confused when he was asked by his team to focus more on Iowa and ignore other states for a while. Obama had to contend with John Edwards and Hillary Clinton, both of them seasoned and experienced politicians.

Politics is a big game. Your strategy may not mean anything if you have no resources to execute it; and so, money comes into importance. Creating and running a system to look after the nationwide campaign needed finances; and Obama found that most of the financial resources were commanded by Hillary, as they were in the business for about three decades and had built up a steady base of financers. Obama felt he could not build up such a vast base, and if he faltered, he would be in no position to remain in contention.

But luck was in his favour. The people were now looking for change, and this hunger for change was stronger than Obama anticipated. People were looking for some fresh air to move into the room through the small vents and cracks and this did not fail to bring in finances, though in small amounts for the initial period. Much of the finance came through the internet, from college students, from grandmas and small workers. The greatest benefit of all this was that his campaign now had the support from the grassroots. The messages accompanying these transactions also supported that they were with him, assuring him that they were on the ground, millions of them, though scattered all over the country. Nothing could be better than this. No leader can be a winner without the grassroots support, and this was coming of its own.

The finance picked up momentum as the time passed, and the finances were well managed under the overall supervision of Penny Pritzker, a businesswoman and a long-time friend from Chicago, and Julianna Smoot.

Winning Iowa was important for the overall victory. It is one of the US states that hold a caucus to determine which candidates their delegates will support. For readers' benefit, a caucus is a meeting to select or promote a candidate. It is unlike traditional primary election in which citizens cast votes and you cannot know who has voted for whom. On the other hand, in a caucus, people gather at an appointed hour at a venue, which may be a public place like a gym or a library, to debate the merit of each candidate, and this process may go on for as long as three hours, or even more, until the gathering comes to a conclusion which candidate they ought to support in the forthcoming elections. As common populace was involved in these caucuses, there was much chance that they would support a better-known candidate like Hillary than Obama; and this was a massive problem to deal with, and they needed to win over the caucus-goers because they played a vital part in forming public opinion about candidates, and this had a deep impact on the final outcome.

To bring the caucuses round to their support, Obama and his team planned for opening a small office, under the command of a young staffer, in each of the 90 counties in Iowa to engineer favourable local political support.

Phrases and slogans enthuse people greatly. They had to spend a lot of time deciding whether they should go for slogans that sounded like the old ones (e.g., Time for Change) to those that touched the sentiments of the young technological minds. And they fell for the one which Tewes authored: RESPECT, EMPOWER, INCLUDE. From the very outset, this motto was appealing as it touched the strings of the heart.

The overall strategy started to concretise benefits in a period of six months; small donations exceeded anticipated amounts and projections, and this enabled the team to go on air with Iowa TV. In June, the school vacation allowed the family to be with Obama, and they took part in road shows and campaigns, building up a favourable atmosphere. In place of organising large crowds, the team decided to manage smaller crowds having a couple of hundred people, which allowed Obama to have a one-to-one talk. This allowed him an insight what was troubling people, and how he could raise those issues, as he did for laid-off workers and took up agri-business concerns. The most important issue came up was that of healthcare, and it laid the foundation which culminated into Obamacare in the later years.

When all these issues came up and Obama started to know about them well enough, he formed concrete ideas about them, and they formed a matter of the heart, and less that of the head. As he included these experiences in his speeches, people felt that he was talking of themselves;

and this led to the evolution of interpersonal emotions, which is so crucial to turn time in one's favour. He had correctly understood the voters' mood that they did not want to listen to the conventional wisdom in a parrot-like fashion. He did not shy away from telling hard truths. For example, when he addressed a gathering of teachers, he supported the cause of higher salaries, and at the same time, spoke of higher accountability for them.

At times, he was given tough alternatives to choose from; like who of Fidel Castro, Mahmoud Ahmadinejad, Kim Jong Il he would like to meet in the first year as the president; he was clear in his approach that he would be open to meet any world leader provided he felt it would further the American interests. Though his contenders were opposed to this standpoint, Obama was sure that he was right as he felt that diplomatic solutions were the most opportune to tackle international problems and conflicts, and America should not shy away from engaging even the adversaries if conflicts could be resolved amicably and to the satisfaction of all, especially America.

This approach allowed Obama to look different from other contenders from his party who viewed that meeting the US President was like a privilege to be earned, but Obama placed the national interests above all of this hoopla.

At this time, the US viewed Pakistan as a reliable partner in its fight against terrorism; however, when Obama was asked in one meeting if he would act if he ever found that Osama bin Laden was located in Pakistani territory, he responded positively that he would. And in the days to come, we would see that he would give a concrete shape to this promise, and it was well applauded the world over; but so was not the case at that time, because the contenders said that Obama was not yet mature enough to be the US president.

Obama was of the clear view that diplomatic options should be explored before taking any military action. And these rational approaches to policy issues brought people to support him, though the electoral pundits thought otherwise. It was a gratifying outcome for him as the contenders seemed to fall out of the race.

With his approach, primary public and media attention in Iowa was turned in favour of Obama; and it boosted his chances to remain in the final fray for presidency. Excessive attention to Iowa did no good so far as his national campaign was concerned. So, now the time was ripe to pay attention to national politics and other states. To his respite, he found that his contenders were floundering on several issues in which a clear stand had to be taken, but they were not willing to do so, and in the process, he had been described as "garden-variety Washington politician" but Obama now started to behave like a seasoned statesman who would display his decisive abilities and views.

Now was the time when he had to beat the contenders from his own party, but also stand against the policies that the Republicans professed. His speeches now dwelt on clear outlines on a variety of issues ranging right from climate change to affordability of healthcare; and how the country needed clear leadership; he said in his speeches that the country needed the leaders who were moved not by polls and politics but by principles, not by calculation but by conviction. With his right word for the right time, he strengthened his position as the Democrat candidate.

Until this time, the contenders had not been taking Obama seriously, so they were focussing attention on other states and when they noticed that he was emerging as a vigorous leader in the race, they changed the tack and went after him. But they committed the mistakes that Modi's opponents did in India. In the US, the contenders raised points revolving around his experience as a leader and his ability to take on the Republican candidate. In some ways, this attack was childish too, as it was also claimed that Obama had ambitions to become the President as a little child when he had written an essay wanting to be the President. People felt that it was going too personal, so support for Obama mounted further. This was chiefly because his campaign was managed different from others'; they consistently emphasised a positive message, highlighting what he stood for rather than what he was against.

As the time passed, the campaign got intense; all contenders, including Obama, trying to put out the best they could, doing every bit in their power and resources. All eyes were now set on Iowa, trying to win any uncommitted voters. At the caucuses, the response was wonderful; and when the results came, they showed Obama winning Iowa decisively, carrying just about every demographic group. The victory was propelled by unprecedented turnout because it was what he had eyed for. The victory in Iowa was described as 'stunning' and 'seismic' by the media, and drew national attention. It was a special case because the entire campaign in Iowa had been built up on personal contacts with the voters, and it signalled a broader appetite for change in the entire country.

Obama won in Iowa and lost in New Hampshire, but he had foreseen it, and was ready to come up with the reasons for this; it only showed that he could stand with adversity in rough times. This stand helped to shore up his campaign in other states, as the support showed in the form of online donations to his cause. Not only this, the governors came out openly in his support. All this gave the impression that he was still in the fray and all was not lost. People described that it was his optimism that carried him through the loss in New Hampshire.

Obama was asked during his campaign the secret behind his ability to maintain composure in the middle of crisis. He said that it might be just a matter of temperament or just because of the fact that he was raised in Hawaii. Then he turns to the fact that it was due to how he trained himself to take the long view about things, and how important it is to remain focussed on your goals rather than getting disturbed by the daily and routine ups and downs that an individual is bound to face in his daily life. IIc also took inspiration from his grandmother, who often guided him how to stay focussed after a disaster. After his defeat in New Hampshire, Obama flew to meet her to find words of inspiration, and she was ever willing to do this without asking for it. She herself had suffered miseries in her life, but nothing had bent her spirit to fight back.

For Obama, it is important to view the entire country as the United States of America, rather than viewing it as a white or a black America, or an America that is inhabited by a specific community. He did not feel it like to address the issues because it could serve the interests of a particular community or section of people. The country is made up of a variety of communities and sections, but they all should come together as citizens of the nation as a whole; the interests of individuals, irrespective of their communities, were important, because when things take to look after interests of a particular community, they often take the form of appeasement, and this results into awkward politics, as happens in a number of countries across the world including India.

The opponents were wont to raise racial issue, especially the colour of the skin that Obama was of, to create an impression of being the 'other', and this issue was hard to tackle, but all sorts of means were being tried to put him down. Not only this, several fly-by-night websites came in hordes to malign his name and race; and even questioned the veracity of his being an American even. They went so low in their claims that declared him to have been schooled in an Indonesian madrassa, and thus, attributed 'foreignness' to him, and also accused that he had dealt in drugs. He was even described as a dad who let bread go stale in the kitchen and left dirty laundry lying around. This is the way political fights become dirty and personal, and it is not easy for anyone to digest such baseless accusations.

Seething under the pain of racialism, Obama continued to put up a brave face. He was committed to not inflict such accusations on his opponents, and this did his cause good.

Not only this, the opponents targeted Michelle too, claiming that she was not the First Lady material. She was being judged from the stereotypes that had been created about the First Lady, in which a black woman did not fit. She was described as one who did not meet the prescribed standards of femininity and physique; she was even described as too loud with hair too nappy, and her personality as more of 'masculine' than 'feminine'. The attacks were becoming too personal, but all this had to be endured.

When you are in public life, a ‘gaffe’ can occur any time, and often they are the result of carelessness. Obama for himself had a team of people to look after his needs and also to keep him in check in his speeches, dresses and behaviour. However, there was no such team to look after Michelle, and it was here that a gaffe occurred when she said in a speech: "For the first time in my adult lifetime, I'm really proud of my country...because I think people are hungry for change". This statement was like the one copied from a textbook, the one that had been uttered several times over by several people in the past. When this statement started to be commented upon in the media, Obama became awarre of Michelle's limitations and took appropriate action about it.

The reporters were trying to exploit this statement trying to blow it out of proportions; all this seemed to be a part of the larger and uglier agenda in order to present a negative portrait of the 'black' Obamas. This concept was being built from the stereotypes, stoked by fear and meant to feed a general nervousness that a black person would be able to make the most important decisions of their life and country, and would be having a black family in the White House. Obama, together with his team, were ready to counter this negative campaign, but he found it hard to assuage the hurt feelings of his wife; nothing seemed to make her feel better.

This was the reason that Obama and his team ducked racial issues, though they spoke in clear terms on issues like immigration reform and civil rights. Being an African-American, often people sympathised with him because of racial injustice was a reality, and this ensured that all blacks were going to vote for him; but this could not be enough to win the elections. So, it was necessary for him to form an image that would attract all segments of people, and this was the reason that he took a rational, national, patriotic stand on all issues concerning the country. Still, there was fear that a white candidate would win most of the votes and might be preferred despite floppy campaign, and this mindset had to be tackled well.

However, hovering over the common and general issues had its own share of risks. Criticisms came up not only from rivals but also friends that an emphasis on universal programmes often meant benefits less directly targeted to those most in need; and this necessitated that the black people did not come out openly in his favour as it would limit his audience; they would have to maintain a stance of optimism and strategic patience before they went all out in his favour.

Many more obstacles had to be tackled before he could win the candidature of his party for the high post. He had originally thought that he was going to win South Carolina with ease as it had a sizeable black population, but by the last week of January, it came out that he did not command support more than 10 percent; but he did not give up hope and worked hard with his team, planning the strategy for the final day. And the result was astonishing; he won in the state because 80 percent of the massive black turnout and 24 percent of the white vote turned in his favour. And now was the time to look to more states.

Gradually, things started to fall in place in favour of Obama; at many places the support was spontaneous and he or his team had not done anything to motivate there. One such state was a small state of Idaho, where he won a decisive victory; it was so important that he gained more delegates there than Hillary got from winning New Jersey, a state with more than five times the population; and this became the pattern everywhere. Thirteen of the twenty-two Super Tuesday contests went his way; overall Obama ended up netting thirteen more delegates than her nearest rival.

Technology was being used by all candidates, but it was a personalised effort in the case of Obama team, because emails and queries were being responded at a personal level, and groups had been formed on social media platforms where discussions were encouraged and a positive opinion was being formulated. While he was happy that technology had come to his rescue because of his limited resources, yet he was pained to note why this technology was not being used to unite the people and serve the national interests in place of creating divisions.

The campaign continued to grow through the hard work that Obama and his team had put up and through the subscriptions that he had received from small donors. There were several glitches during the course of the campaign, and they led to formulating rules, protocols, processes and hierarchies in which to operate. At this stage, over one thousand people had been working in different capacities in his nationwide team. Having a larger team had its negative aspects too, as there were fewer people who addressed him as 'Barack' and more people calling him 'sir' or 'senator'. With his old team, all were habituated of him being around, but now the trend had changed. Whenever he entered a room, the staff would shuffle out thinking that he must not be disturbed. And when he said that they could stick around, they would behave as if a big boss was around. This made him feel lonely even in a crowded hall.

The crowds which once had started from a few dozen people now swelled to have thousands of people, often ten thousand or more. At places, the crowd was thirty thousand strong. During these speeches, all care was taken to present a presentable Obama, right from his clothing to make-up to words, so that nothing malfunctioned and a positive impression was given.

After his speeches, Obama often entered the rope line to shake hands, take pictures and share a brief talk with the howling masses. People wanted to touch him, shake hands with him and often pass some messages written on a piece of paper. He often wondered if he would ever be able to be so close to people once he was President, because the protocols would not allow him to be so frank to people.

As the nomination time neared, all kinds of restrictions had been imposed on him. His world shrank as government staff blended themselves with his staff and they would not be distinguishable. Now, he was no longer free to do whatever he felt like, spontaneity just evaporated from his life. He was now not allowed to interact with strangers or walk through a grocery store. He once described all these restrictions like a 'circus cage' imposed on a 'dancing bear'. Sometimes, he escaped these restrictions to take part in some public shows, but these were fully controlled by the time the winter in 2008 set in; the bear had finally been taught how to be in captivity without raising objections.

All this hard work had been into the primary contest, and nomination as a Democrat candidate was still away by a few weeks. On the other hand, John McCain was going to be a Republican candidate at least by a couple weeks earlier than him. This simply meant that he would be able to have enough time to lay the foundation of his presidential campaign while Obama was still facing uncertainties whether he would be able to make it. This could be a big setback.

Before this setback could be tackled, there was another massive obstacle that could prove very crucial to the very survival of Obama as a Democrat candidate. This situation arose from a video of reverend Jeremiah Wright, Obama's black pastor. The ABC News had compiled a series of short clips culled from several years of his sermons into a video in which he was shown describing anti-American sentiments, offending people, especially the whites. The video did not take much time before it became viral, and it was sure to hurt, nay destroy the very campaign.

It is a fact that despite America being a free-thinking country, the people felt otherwise when it came to racial issues, as the blacks are often considered the 'other'. This video needed to be tackled as it could not be condemned as Obama having nothing to do with it, because Wright was his pastor; and this had to be done wisely and prudently. He sat down with his team dictating the important points that his speech should include to contest the claims, and he did this with his natural flow. He went on to describe how Wright was a representative of America's racial legacy, how bitterness is harboured by people and institutes based on racial traits, and how they feel betrayed by a country they are citizens of. Then he set his eyes on the other side, and went on to explain why the whites would resist, or even resent claims of injustice from the blacks. All whites are not racists. He emphasised that this shortcoming in the mind could not be overcome unless all people came to know of the reality that the other side viewed, and it was essential to solve the problem that the country faced. A stronger America could emerge only if all communities lived in harmony with mutual understanding. He went on to describe an incident in which he was made to feel bad because he had a different skin colour; but this could not be the basis of the national abuse. These were not the only roadblocks, there were others too, and some of them were of Obama's making himself. These already had made a dent in the support base, and it was sure that if no effort was made to set the things right, the damage could cost him the nomination.

Speaking with genuine sincerity and passion for commitment at the next venue, Obama won the hearts of the people, though the Wright video had harmed his interests in Pennsylvania. Still, he continued to win endorsements from people. He himself spoke to Wright over phone and sought clarification; and he said that the reporters had not bothered to listen to his full speeches, rather they had created the video from the small narrations that suited their interest. He questioned how his entire life's sermons be squeezed into a two-minute video.

To make matters worse, Wright appeared before the press, and when strafed by political questions, his patience gave way and he declared America to be a racist country. This was the worst that Obama's campaign could suffer, and something had to be done if he had to win nomination followed by the general election.

Obama issued a brief statement unequivocally denouncing and separating himself from Reverend Wright. The matter was as good as solved now. At least, the reporters would not chase him down with his comments on this issue. No further damage from this incident was expected to come now. It was once again that he now focussed on issues concerning healthcare, Iraq war and other things touched the popular psyche.

What people like in a leader is his decision-making ability, even if the decision goes against themselves. We have seen Modi's rising popularity despite a number of harsh decisions he has taken. And such an issue came up before Obama during the last leg of his election campaign when the gas prices had been skyrocketing, and people were feeling bad all about this. The contenders John McCain and Hillary proposed a tax deduction to ease out the situation, but Obama thought otherwise. Cutting down on gas tax appeared to him a superficial appeal because it would drain an already depleted federal highway fund, leading to fewer infrastructure projects and jobs; while the motorists would not see much of benefit because the gas station owners were not likely to pass the benefit to consumers for more than a few cents. The proposal to tax deduction was actually a situation in which the problem would remain unsolved or rather get further vitiated.

Obama held a press conference and stated that he preferred, instead of a political posturing designed to give the impression of action without actually solving the problem, to go for a serious long-term energy policy. This stand was like depriving the voters some crucial money. The contenders immediately made the case in their favour what a few hundred dollars could mean to a working family. In response, Obama went for an ad on the issue in which national interest was presented.

Not everybody was sure if this stance would prove in his favour, but it did. And the outcome was that Obama won North Carolina by fourteen points and pulled out an effective tie in Indiana, losing by just a few thousand votes. This also ensured that he was going to be the Democrat nominee for President, with Hillary bowing out of the contest on a gracious note. At the Democratic Convention Center in Denver, Colorado, Hillary asked her supporters to endorse Obama, and she and Bill Clinton gave convention speeches in his support.

On the other hand, Obama gave his acceptance speech not at the Democratic Convention Center but at Invesco Field at Mile High, and to listen to him on this occasion were present eighty-four thousand people; and the speech was viewed by more than three million people across the globe. Though six more rounds of contests still remained, but the results clearly announced that the race for nomination was virtually over. With this, now was the time to pay attention to the general elections that were on the horizon, because there was not much time to waste.

❑❑

The Contest for Presidency

The battle for nomination was virtually over in which Obama took a clear lead, though the results were a few days away. The crucial question was not whether he would make a good president, it was whether the American people were ready to place their faith in a young and inexperienced man who evoked interest yet spoke on issues that hinged more on national interest rather than personal welfare issues; who had sympathies with people but placed national interests above anything else. Moreover, he, in his campaign, had given people much cause to resent and not support him in the general election. Despite all this, people had cultivated interest and likeness in him, and had accepted his call for something different.

It was now time for Obama to think about the broader question and design his broader electoral strategy for the general election. The crucial question for the big post was to get the requisite 270 electoral votes, in face of the perennial situation that the majority of states were either Republican or Democratic, and a party nominee could easily sail through the respective states supporting him/her.

An important lesson that Obama and his team had drawn from the nationwide primary campaign was that they had created a team of trusted volunteers in several states, including those in Republican states, that the past Democrats had not done earlier. Bringing their heads together with his team members, they were set to take an unconventional approach, that was to compete in the Republican-leaning states, the states which were thought unconquerable by Democrats and which had not fallen to the Democrats in decades. As they looked at the western states like Colorado and Nevada, the chances seemed bright that they could muster strength from them. All through the primary campaign, Obama had leaned on the youths, and this could have a positive impact even in these states.

This strategy was good and seemed effective, because it would lead to multiple openings for support from people. A vital advantage of this approach would be that the rivals would have to concentrate more on their support states and this would compel them to leave out the traditional Democrat states in order to keep their Republican states under their armpit.

Obama had to contest with John McCain, the Republican candidate. The fun was that even Obama considered him most worthy of the prize and admired him. He was a volatile person who could put up a strong fight and had a reputation to rely on because of his past as a navy pilot who had lived five years and a half as a POW but never lost his esteem and courage. Moreover, he was a sensible politician who could thwart his own party's line when it came to stand for national issues, including those on immigration and climate change. Obama has described him as 'insightful and self-deprecating'. The great thing about him in the Senate was that he would puncture pretension and hypocrisy arising from either side of the aisle. It was due to this image that he was often called a Republican only in name. The fight was going to be tough, and Obama was mentally ready for the contest.

In contrast to John McCain, Obama was inexperienced, he had not served in the military or even in an executive office, and he was an African-American. The first question was that of acceptability, and the remaining was dependent on how he fared on the national issues, especially those which concerned the conflicts in other countries including Iraq and Afghanistan. To see the ground situation himself, Obama set out on a nine-day foreign tour, when he paid brief visits to a number of countries including Kuwait, Afghanistan, Iraq, Israel, Jordan, Britain, Germany and France. During this visit, he explained his position to the press and even delivered a keynote address in Berlin. This showed how he could deal with the complicated issues that faced the world, and also gave him an opportunity to highlight the strained alliances that had come up during the Bush administration.

This international visit was a risky one, because if he floundered even on one occasion, that might be taken to mean that he was completely out of the sync and was incapable of dealing with the foreign relations that are so crucial in the national life of the US. It was like a tightrope walk. However, he flew back to America with flying colours and confident that he could be a diplomatic success and world leader.

It was also the time to decide who his running mate would be, who would ultimately become the Vice President in case the election brought favourable results. He narrowed down to two: Governor Tim Kaine of Virginia and Senator Joe Biden of Delaware. The latter was destined to take oath as the President in 2021. Obama felt himself closer to Tim Kaine as the two were same age, while Biden was nineteen years his senior. While other particulars were common for Obama and Kaine, Biden was an experienced guy with thirty-five years in the Senate, during this period he had also served in important capacities including as the chairman of the Judiciary Committee and the Foreign Relations Committee.

As Obama looked at the two more closely, he found that Biden was a temperamentally cool and collected personality, with a lot of warmth and little inhibition; and he loved to share what came up his mind. His greatest trait was that he loved to be in company with a perennial smile adorning his pretty face. Whenever Biden was in others' company, he would find one or the other way to commend and admire others; he would admire the place they belonged, or their parents or children, or even profession. Wherever he went, he would be indulging himself in lavish handshakes, hugs and kisses. He was ready to compliment each and every person, and this brought a lot of support for him.

Like any person, Biden had his shortcomings, and that was, he was too verbose; he talked incessantly; his speeches often ran beyond the prescribed limits. However, overall, he was a likeable guy and his strengths far outweighed his shortcomings. He possessed a deep understanding of the national and international issues, and could present his point effectively, and that was an important trait for a leader.

Early in life, soon after Biden had been elected to the Senate, he had suffered a terrible incident in which his wife and baby daughter had been killed in a car accident, and his two young sons were injured. He overcame this catastrophe with the help of his second wife, and provided support and care to the injured children.

Seeing his strengths, Obama proposed to Biden to join him in the fray as his running mate. Naturally, being senior, it was a difficult proposition for him to play second fiddle to someone who was junior to him, but he did consent on the condition that he would be the last voice in the room whenever any issue came up, and he committed that he would stand by and defend any decision that Obama took in the capacity of the President. Taking him in was advantageous for Obama too, because taking Kaine could mean that both were inexperienced, and they could cause a change that could be too unexpected. Youthfulness combined with experience, that was what the Democratic team made up.

The rival in the general election for presidency was John McCain, and he had secured his Republican nomination three months before Obama, yet he had not utilised this gap to gain a lead over him. In any election, it is the swing voters that matter most, and in this case, McCain had not done much to convince them to his side; so the perspective was wide open for Obama to target these unpersuaded people. He started his campaign with a magnificent speech in the Democratic National

Convention, and in a survey, it came up that he gained a five-point lead over his rival soon after it.

For McCain, the challenge was too big, because he had to emerge out of George Bush's shadow, who was struggling in view of the unpopular Iraq war, climate change and immigration issues; and he found it hard to promise a change in his approach, which could immediately rubbish the Republican stand on them and render the Bush administration unpopular.

Obama felt an early shock on hearing about McCain's running mate; she was Sarah Palin, the forty-four-year-old governor of Alaska. She could be a disrupter for him because she was young and a woman, and her resume made her a perfect white working American who could muster support from the working classes. She was a delight to watch when she spoke on the stage; she fascinated people with her style and words. However, what worked against her was that she did not possess a deep understanding of the national and international issues, and she was little known at the national level. While Obama had an experienced mate to consult on issues he could flounder on, McCain would have none of such a person, and that was a massive shortcoming for him.

When Obama had started with his campaign, Iraq war had been the biggest issue, though even then he had stressed on paying more attention to economic policies which should be guided to progressive aspect for a change.

And by this time, global and technological factors had been causing a basic change in the American economy, especially due to outsourcing of jobs due to availability of low-cost labour; the production undertaken overseas led to cheaper goods to be sold by big-box retailers; and this posed an inequitable situation for the small businesses. Technology had played the culprit in which entire office work had been outsourced in several cases; and some whole industries had been shut down.

This situation was very favourable to those who had deep pockets, but it presented a harsh situation for ordinary workers, as they now found themselves on a weak note when it came to bargaining pay and other perks, as the number of layoffs increased. Wages became stagnant and benefits were reduced for them. All this while, general living, education and healthcare became gradually costlier, putting the financial burden on common people. Decreased income takes its first toll on the things and facilities which are considered avoidable, such as prep classes, sports camps, internships, but which are vital for personality building. This also brings an element of inequality in the society, which even otherwise was high, and it could have made things worse for people.

Obama felt that this situation had arisen due to faulty economic policies which had started from the time of Ronald Reagan. Privatisation was the culprit, he felt, because the federal budget targeted less on common welfare measures such as child education to infrastructure; and in case of any financial turbulence, people were bound to leave out the amenities which might come to be considered inevitable, resulting into massive inequality creating high and low societies. As money was saved on these essential basic things, the rich had been allowed tax cuts.

Obama further felt that the prevailing economic policies needed to be guided in proper direction in place of replacing them with radical things which could leave only a temporary but lasting negative impact. In the modern world, it was no more possible to stop automation or global reach; this could have great repercussions. Obama felt that there was need to raise taxes for the rich so that the drive for infrastructure investment could be infused with vigour; but talking of raising taxes in the election campaign could backfire. Even then, he felt that it was worth the risk as the money got from the rich could be well utilised in providing investments in education, research and infrastructure. He promised that he would take steps to strengthen unions and raise the minimum wage, with emphasis on universal healthcare and make education more affordable right from elementary school to college.

When Obama started to speak in the favour of what he felt, there were many takers. He was a little scared that the rich could influence the common people away from supporting him, but he found that even they were supportive of his policies. He foresaw that strong labour laws would help build a thriving middle class raising the consumption level doing overall good to economy; all this while, strong action needed to be taken against unsafe products and fraudulent schemes, which could be brought under the scanner of consumer welfare and protection schemes.

While his talk was being accepted for its benefits, the economy was falling viciously, and the development on Wall Street had started to spin out of control because several financial institutes had begun to falter and go broke or face massive problems. A sort of financial panic was ensuing and it was bound to impact good as well as bad businesses, big as well as small businesses. The country was in a recession, a massive one. Structural weakness of the American economy was out on the prowl taking toll on housing prices, tightening credit, declining stock market, leading to laying off workers and cancellation of business orders. The panic spread all over. People were forced to sell their luxuries and sit without work; payrolls were cut and spending went down drastically. The demand contracted and the situation deteriorated gradually in the months to come. Unemployment was at its worst in twenty years. The rescue package did not work due to rising gas prices.

Economic slowdown put Obama in a stronger place vis-à-vis the Republican McCain because he was forced to acknowledge and support Bush's economic policies and rescue packages for banks and financial institutes, as going against the administration could prove quite costly to both the government and his own chances at hustings, so his advisors were pitching for the point to go against the government's policies.

The developing situation was sure to worsen McCain's chances, and Obama could exploit the situation to his advantage. Obama, however, decided to be with the nation. The stakes were high but he decided to do whatever was necessary for the nation, and politics should not become a shelter for poor policies, and he decided to support the government to help it stabilise the situation. Thus, ironically, the candidate of the party in power was going to oppose his own government's policies, while the candidate of the party in opposition was going to support the government on this score.

Economy continued in the free fall mode with more financial institutes facing the worst situation that could ever be imagined.

When the government announced a $700 billion bailout package for economy, McCain first opposed it and then supported it, and thus created a blunder by his own confusion, and this was in the favour of Obama. Taking advantage of this situation, he declared that this zig-zag way of working was leading to the crisis and could better be called 'Bush-McCain' economic agenda in which everything was as opaque as the economy. Despite all this, Obama took care to ensure that his criticism was not so severe as to jeopardise the very rescue package; he only wanted to pass the message of his stand, and did not want the country to suffer on account of his opposition.

While the economic situation was worsening despite the package, the time had come for the first open debate with McCain. He closed himself in the hotel room for three days with his specialist staff and advisors to decide on the issues that he would be taking up, because the debate was a vital instrument in bringing home the points he could make.

It was also the time for the passage of the bill granting $700 billion aid, called TARP Act. Both Democrat and Republican senators were raising doubts and objections to it, and it seemed unlikely that it could be passed because the Republicans did not have sufficient votes to ensure its passage, and despite their opposition and objections, they were supposed to support and vote for it. Obama honestly felt that the Democrats needed to support the package else the country was sure to feel the heat. The stakes were high with this unpopular legislation, an election fast approaching and none of the parties willing to give the other something that could be used against it.

Obama thought out a way, and that was to take politics out of this issue. He discussed with his staff if he and McCain could issue a joint statement supporting the bailout package, else the economy was bound to fall in severe depression. The only hitch was whether McCain would be supportive of the idea, and fortunately, he was. Of course, he wanted to do it in another way, and he was mulling over an idea to suspend the election campaign until the package was passed. The Indian political leaders have a lesson to learn from this. Here in India, leaders support or oppose any idea or bill, whether good or bad for the country, primarily keeping their political interests and vote-banks in view.

You might think that the western people are not superstitious and orthodox, but ironically, the truth is otherwise. During the course of his election campaign, Obama had collected an assortment of charms and this collection kept rising, and these included not only the Christian symbols, but also those from other faiths and religions. On any given day, he would choose a few of these charms and keep them in his pocket, and if the day went good, he would keep in mind which variety he was carrying that day, and often made sure that he carried the same group again. These charms included a miniature Buddha, a tiny bronze Hanuman, several angels, rosary beads, crystals and rocks. He admits that he was unsure if these charms benefited or raised his chances to success, but he figured out that they caused no harm to him. He says that he felt comforted when he touched them or turned them over in his palms, when light jangling raised his spirits.

Obama also grew somewhat superstitious about songs. Before his meeting people or speaking at an event, he would glance over the notes about the points he needed to make, and he would avail this opportunity to listen to some songs, for which he carried either earbuds or a small portable speaker. He became somewhat compulsive about hearing certain songs, which included jazz classics and raps; and he chose the ones which provided him motivation. He could also be seen nodding his head and beating his shoe lightly against the floor of the van in which he travelled to events. Music put him in right mood.

The crucial question was if these superstitions worked in his favour. Obama recollects the time when he went for the first debate with McCain towards the close of September. As he readied to go on to the stage, he ate his favourite food (steak), again a superstition, listened to music and jingled his charms in his pocket. I am not sure whether these superstitions worked in his favour, but certainly, McCain was facing the heat at the hands of the reporters who had been asking hard questions over the declining economy, and he was finding it hard to put his case to them. As he faltered, Obama's case strengthened, and I again doubt if this was due to his taking shelter to superstitions.

The debate went well, and was instrumental in turning in the voters who were yet undecided whom to choose between them. The post-debate survey showed Obama on a high note. The good job was done and now there was a need to sustain this positive outcome, but that would require a huge effort.

Back to economic depression, the TARP bill fell in the House of Representatives, and funnily, two-thirds of the Democrats voted in support of it while two-thirds of Republicans voted against it. The Dow Jones suffered a terrifying 778 points in a single day. Of course, an amended rescue package had to be passed a few days later because that was the need of the hour. But it had a positive impact for Obama as now McCain was seen as the one who could not be trusted to handle the crisis of that size and extent.

Despite this lead and favourable popular opinion, Obama could not afford to lower his guard, and he continued to work hard in his campaign, visiting towns and cities and states, and also made a point to be in personal touch with as many people as may be possible, because he would not be able to do so in a few days when the state security would creep in as he could likely be the next President and the government could not relax about any security threat that might be looming large over his head. Still, Obama enjoyed some traditional campaigning styles in which he met people on the roadside, and knocked at doors, and visited restaurants and joints to give autographs.

Normally, personal attacks are the norms during an election in several countries, including ours, but that was not the case between Obama and McCain. Both of them respected each other and said good things about each other, and backed away whenever any attempt was made to vitiate the atmosphere. In one election meeting, an announcer cried into the microphone that he was afraid of Obama as the President, McCain immediately retorted that he is a decent person and he could not be scared as the President. The two candidates from different parties respected each other. Again, we in India have a crucial lesson to learn from this.

Obama was careful that no hype was created about him, and that the idea of 'him' was far inferior to the idea of 'we' (the Americans). All this while, despite the passage of the TARP Act, the economy remained in a bad shape, and it would be a tumultuous task for Obama to take on when he would be administered oath of office.

And finally, it was the election day. It is the time when lull pervades the atmosphere, just like antithesis of the noise and hullabaloo of the election speeches, movements, interviews, and what not. But this lull is normally like the quiet that is often experienced just before a tempest. But there is a flurry of activity, all subdued in silence as if everybody is out there doing his bit to contribute to the democratic process. There are no ads and noise, but there are volunteers who are silently attempting to bring out the voters from the comfort of their houses, especially in the areas where supporters live. Sometimes, these volunteers have to face a tricky task as voters often ask what is there to vote for, and they have to convince the high points of the respective candidate.

There may be all-pervasive lull, but so is not the case with the mind of the candidates. They are filled with doubt, suspicion, rumours; they are unendingly scurrying for field reports on their phones and laptops, trying to keep pace with what is happening in the election booths. Obama too cast his vote along with his family, and then went out to play badminton, once again a form of superstition evolved in the process.

Waiting for the election result is more anxious and strenuous period rather than exciting; it becomes exciting only when favourable reports pour in; and there was time for that to occur. With voting still in full swing, there were reports that turnout was really good, shattering records across the country. The queues were so long at places that voters had to wait for a few hours before their turn came to cast the vote. And as specialists tell, such a high turnout occurs when people are vying for change or are supporting the existing government; but the latter could not be the case in view of the fact that economy was in a really bad shape, and Bush administration was not likely to get such a massive support. It simply meant that Obama's agenda had made the masses jubilant.

The administration too had seen the change coming in, as security for Obama and his family was stepped up, and as they drove along Lake Michigan, no other cars could be seen on the road other than Obama's cavalcade and Malia was quick to point it out.

As Obama and his family relaxed waiting for the things to unfold, the TV continued to show the latest news around the country, and the entire focus was shifted to election. And then suddenly, the face of Obama appeared on ABC News and the accompanying announcement declared that he was going to be the forty-fourth president of the United States. The room erupted in jubilation. The hard work over the past two years had paved in the path to success. And it was no ordinary one; a black African-American was going to be the next President, the most powerful person on the earth.

Again, there was an instance which our politicians need to learn from America. John McCain called and congratulated Obama in graceful words; he emphasised how history had been created and also promised to help him prove a good president. Democracy was breathing life into its most spectacular form. As I write these lines, I feel a kind of excitement building within me; perhaps it is owing to the fact that an unlikely person was now going to enter the White House and sit in the Oval Office, and he had risen from very ordinary background. There is much motivation to be drawn from this; his campaign had not been flawless, but he was ever prepared to amend himself and mould himself and think deeper how he could come out the winner, and in this process, his prudent and able staff achieved what was unimaginable. Of course, the swearing-in would take another three months, during which the remaining electoral processes would be undertaken and the result would be announced formally.

To sum up the election, Obama won the presidency with 365 electoral votes as against 173 received by McCain. He won 52.9% of the popular vote to McCain's 45.7%. He made his victory speech before thousands of supporters at Grant Park in Chicago.

❑❑

Taking on the World

As the President-elect, the first challenge that Obama was to face was to form his team. The important point was whom to include in his team that would enable him to bring out the policies that could implement his ideology and bring relief to important issues of economic depression, climate change, national security and the ever lingering problem of terrorism. Making an announcement is not so easy as task as it might be thought. Each person who might be considered for a post has a history of his own, with his own strengths and weaknesses, and a set of supporters and opponents, and a decision is required to be made in the best interests of the country and the party.

Whenever an appointment is made, the President's political intentions are questioned, long debates are conducted in the media if the decision was leaning to the right or to the left, or the centrist approach had been preferred. And the critical media was sure to prove that each appointment he made was not eligible and suitable for the job. Each appointment brings out the fact what is to unfold in the near future in policy terms. Only selecting people for appointments is not the only problem, leaving out the people from appointments is equally a daunting task, as there are people who think themselves to be the fittest for the post, and these are the people who are out to spoil the game.

The intervening period, until Obama took the oath of office, was to be utilised in forming his team. He had to take into consideration a number of factors including aspirations, country's needs, people's desires and smooth administration. So, he decided to go for a mixed team having experience and novelty, budding youthfulness under the guidance of grey hair.

Despite the TARP and the measures taken under it, the economy remained in its grim shape as the banks and financial institutions were on the verge of collapse, and the rate of unemployment was rising constantly. He did not have the option of reinventing economy as the world economy was in a disastrous shape; rather his first priority was to prevent the further disaster. This was going to be a crucial test for his administration, so he opted for experience over aspirations or any other factor. He chose not one but two to do this task; they were Larry Summers and Tim Geithner; the former as the dircctor of the National Economic Council (NEC) and the latter as the Treasury Secretary.

There were numerous other challenges too, like the volatile international situation marred by terrorism and imperialistic ambitions by a few countries. There was a sizeable number of American troops stationed abroad; there were almost 180,000 troops in Iraq and Afghanistan, leave the others. This was a sizeable number. When they entered these territories, Obama had opposed but now it could not be so easy to pull them out leaving the fine job that they had been doing out there. This was the reason that he decided to continue with Bob Gates as the Secretary of Defense, because a change of guard at this juncture could prove catastrophic for the US forces, and this was a sentimental issue in the country, especially in view of the casualties that were caused there. Moreover, it was a viable political move, because it would ensure continuity in policy and at the same time, would offset the stand taken by Obama in his early election campaign that he was opposed to invasion in Iraq; moreover, he had never served in uniform. This would also help him overcome his biases against the military strategy abroad.

Taking in Gates as the Secretary of Defense was like taking in a rival; Obama described this strategy as 'team of rivals', and his choice was not limited to only Gates; he was now looking for more rivals, and this time he found Hillary Clinton whom he wanted to appoint as the secretary of state; she was the same rival who had run against her for the Democratic nomination. Though his advisors advised against this, Obama was in particular impressed by her intelligence, preparation and work ethic; she was a patriot to the core and was fully committed to the cause whichever she took up during the course of her work. He refused in the beginning, but constant wooing made her decide in favour.

One thing that Obama could make out clearly was that choosing one from a horde of contenders for any post was not an easy task. He spent countless hours discussing and thinking who should be appointed what; each appointment had to be done with an eye on the policy that he was going to implement in the days to come, and it was not so easy to ignore recommendations that often came.

With his team in place, Obama was looking forward to the D Day - January 20, 2009. The intervening period was no less challenging for him. He was sorting the names for his cabinet, while he had to prepare his inaugural speech as well.

On this day, he woke up well in time, took a run on the treadmill, had shower, shaved and took breakfast before getting into the car with Michelle and headed to the church before they could reach the venue for inaugural. At this time, there was a perception of a terrorist attack at the hands of four Somali youths, so security was beefed up and an evacuation plan was put in place.

They next headed to the White House, and in the company of his important secretaries, incumbent vice president, past presidents and the present President. Obama and Michelle made for the Capitol. It was the first time when he rode in the black limousine better known as 'the Beast'. This special car in which the US presidents travel is a mobile arsenal designed to survive even a bomb blast, and had inbuilt facilities which could be compared with the best in terms of luxury, security and functioning.

As the motorcade rolled, the crowds lined on either side of the streets cheering the new leader. There were a few people too who protested and shouted slogans against the outgoing President. The job of the President is far bigger than these welcome shouts or protests, and it is better to overlook them and concentrate on the job. For now, everything was set for the oath of office preceded by a prayer. After he delivered his speech and highlighted important points he would like to implement in the years to come during his tenure; the ceremony came to an end and saw Bush and his wife departing for the last time.

Settling down in the White House is as cumbersome as one can face in any other house, and in some ways, it could be more complicated too; because one has to learn how to operate the new types of gadgets and telephones for different needs, and how security issues have to be tackled. It is an overwhelming experience for the new entrants.

Media persons is a necessary appendage for the president, they would be poking noses in whatever was possible and which concerned him including any of his appointments in the personal capacity, such as taking his wife on a date or visiting the field to see his daughters play. Obama objected that the press should be kept away from such personal movements, but then his staff advised against it because the media could then go after the girls, whose privacy was very important; on the other hand, he was leading a public life, and ought to have nothing to hide from the public eye.

The US President is undoubtedly the most powerful person in the world who keeps talking about freedoms and rights, but when it comes to his own freedom and rights, he is more like a parrot in the cage. He is not allowed to keep a personal device for any personal communication. Obama wanted to have a personal device, and he was given something which could be called a 'luxury' for him;

he was given a new Blackberry device, duly approved by his cybersecurity team after weeks of negotiations. This device enabled him to send or receive emails only from 20 contacts; and the microphone and headphone jack had been removed from it; when it was first given him, he looked at it with screwed eyes and described as a toy phone given to a toddler to play. All his contact with the outside world was through the three aides who occupied the outer Oval office.

Obama has ability to vividly describe every person, situation or thing he comes across. And he has described these three aides very interestingly; he has described them as his 'unofficial gatekeepers and personal life-support system'. He has an excellent sense of humour when he says that they ought to be 'telling when I'd spilled soup on my tie, enduring my rants and bad jokes'. Not only these three, he has described almost all staffers in the White House in very colourful words right from the gardener to the photographer who kept constant company with him. In his autobiography, he has also described his residence in the White House as less of a home and more of a boutique hotel equipped with all facilities that could be thought of including gym, pool, tennis court, movie theatre, salon, bowling alley and medical office. There were adequate number of staffers to look after each and every need that might arise right from a small malfunctioning in the switch board to changing flowers in rooms. He has jokingly remarked that his staff was so perfect that it helped him improve his general appearance and also helped his marriage. All these facilities and staff were there to help him present himself in the best of American traditions and also do his work what he was supposed to do as the President.

With the swearing in, Obama was ready for his new role, and the first thing for him was to give a relook on the promises that he had made during his long election campaign, first to win the Democratic nomination, and then for the general election. It was his moral duty to fulfil most of, if not all, the promises that he had made in the process. After all, these are the promises on the basis of which a leader is elevated to an office, and the office now he occupied is seen with curious eyes not only across the country but across the globe.

Many of these promises could be fulfilled by a mere stroke of the pen, through signing orders and ordinances. He started out his term with the signing of an executive order banning torture in prisons and detention centres, and tightening restrictions on lobbyists. And then he turned his attention to his primary interest, to look after the healthcare segment, and for the beginning, he paid attention to children's health insurance programme, followed by granting an incentive for research in the field of embryonic stem-cell.

Obama had of course to wait for nine days before signing his first law, and this law pertained to giving equal wages to men and women for the same work. The law, titled the Lilly Ledbetter Fair Pay Act, was so called after the name of a woman who had worked in a company and was paid routinely less than her male counterparts. In one stroke, much of discrimination had been done away with, and this brought him accolades. Interestingly, this woman had been denied this right by the Supreme Court describing her case as time barred because she failed to file a case for several years from the time the discrimination first occurred.

Enacting a law is a long-drawn affair as much procedure has to be followed in the Congress, but achieving success in less important cases like these gave him confidence that he could well achieve what he had been elected for. And now the time had come to look at major issues which included healthcare, immigration reform and climate change issues. And the biggest problem before them was the collapsing economy, which was no longer limited to only Wall Street. Its repercussions were felt all across the spectrum as people no longer chose to spend which could kickstart the economy; and on the other hand, mounting losses to the bank had kept them away from lending. And this was showing a drastic impact on companies and retailers, while lay-offs became the norm of the day. It was the most terrible recession since 1930s; the rate of unemployment rising unprecedentedly.

The steps needed to be taken immediately, and Obama sat with team for over three hours to determine the strategy he should follow. They zeroed in on three major points: one was to reverse the cycle of contracting demand, for which the option of reducing interest rates was considered which would make everything right from homes to cars to appliances cheaper. However, this option could not be chosen as the interest rates were already close to zero, and could not be further lowered without causing further hurt to the financial system. Another option was for the government to give out a package, that was to pump more money into the system, so that the people looked more confident and started to make financial dealings on a more frequent basis. To solve this, the option to provide stimulus was chosen, and for this an ambitious several hundred-billion-dollar package was considered, but the question remained on which sector should such a massive spending be made. And the third point was to formulate strategy how the bill for stimulus package could be passed through the Congress, which was not functioning well. The term 'stimulus package' was thought not to the likeness of people, so the bill for this was named the American Recovery and Reinvestment Act, comprising a whopping $800 billion package, divided into three buckets; the first was to give direct aid to states and supplement insurance scheme; the second was to give cuts in taxes; and these two buckets ensured that money was delivered in the pockets of people directly; and the third was to go for the infrastructure projects that would bolster employment. It was taken in consideration to start such infrastructure projects that would benefit the people at the local level.

The discussion we have described in the previous two paragraphs took place before Obama entered office, in the capacity of the President-elect, but these proposals were turned down by the Bush administration. As the economy was in a bad shape, the early part of his presidentship was substantially engaged in tackling it and bringing it to an optimum level because there were other pressing issues to focus on too. Let us not forget that a decision by a political leader can seldom go without the opposition's criticism; it is more so in our country, and is present in all other countries in varying degrees, including the US, though maybe on a smaller scale. The planned Recovery Act was of tremendous size and was aimed at averting layoffs, hiring of new workers and promoting green economy. Despite the opposition's criticism on several counts, the Recovery Act garnered popular support, and it got through the Senate, with the grand hope that the economy would start to work again.

As he planned how to bring succour to the people, Obama was flooded with emotional letters from people how they were facing the outcome of the bad economy. He kept awake late into the night, sometimes into the wee hours of the morning, thinking how he could bring succour to people. Working as a night owl gave him the quietest hours at work, and he has described these hours as the most productive hours of the day; it gave him time to catch up on work and prepare himself for whatever was coming next.

Being the President brought a great number of privileges, but the pressure of work was no less. He had to deal with several routine things each day, including intelligence briefings, legislative proposals, drafts of speeches, press conference, talking points on daily basis; and then there were other pressing issues that the world could throw up at any time of day or night. He also ensured that he read a few letters from people, as it made him feel the seriousness of his job most acutely. He read these letters as they gave him an insight what people were feeling that he served. Often, the letters brought suggestions that were very valuable. It also brought the trust that he carried for the people. Not all letters could be sent to the President, as there were bag-loads of them, so he had instructed his staff to send him ten a day. He had specifically instructed them that the letters should be representative of cross sections, and not merely those that supported his ideas. Thus, we can see that he was not averse to receiving criticism of what he was doing in the great chair. The staff had complete freedom to choose which mails or letters would form part of the folder that went to him.

Obama recalls that the letters he received in the first week were mostly congratulatory or feel-good ones, and a few suggestions for legislation, including those from children who wanted reduced homework. With time, the letters became more sombre, narrating personal problems or what they felt like in the contemporary nation and world. Some letters depicted sentiments as they were very angry on what was going on in the country, and some very happy with some actions being taken to improve upon the conditions. Some were written in anger or in desperation, while some of the writers wrote quite in detail about what they wanted and how it could be achieved. One thing is sure in any country: none of your decisions can be accepted by each one of the countrymen; criticism will be there, and it is the root of the democratic system; democracy thrives because there is scope for critique.

In the process of giving aid to overcome the economic crisis, Obama faced hard-hitting reality too. When he allowed the banks to give relief to those customers whose home loans could not be paid in time, there were a number of people who claimed that this step was motivated by racism, as people of certain races were to benefit more from it. He was blamed of 'reverse racism' in which minorities play the race card to get an unfair advantage. Doesn't it sound like 'appeasement' back at home?

Obama also made sure to reply to some of these letters which he felt ought to be replied. Whenever he did so, he would emboss the note with the presidential seal enclosing a detailed reply on what the government was doing to ease the tough situation, though he left writing the detailed answer to his staff. It is a good way of interacting with the people. I found its reflection in Narendra Modi back home when I received a birthday card from him on one occasion and a detailed letter when I gave up LPG subsidy. This immediately brings the leader closer to people as personal sentiments get attached.

His aid was not at all aimed at doing any discrimination, even the facts were otherwise; nonetheless he could not avoid these accusations, as he himself belonged to the coloured community. He asked himself if the country and Americans had actually come a long way off those past times when the property-holding white men deemed it democracy when they were able to acquire more and more of property and holding the blacks as their chattel. It had led to a bloody civil war because the blacks had felt a couple of centuries ago that the liberty of the white people had involved their own subjugation. Obama felt restless that people's minds had not changed much over the centuries. The idea of the government has changed over all these decades; now the government interferes virtually in every sphere of life, including providing relief to people who lose their jobs out of economic crisis, or to victims of natural disasters. Not only this, it has also to undertake welfare measures which includes providing basic facilities to even in the remotest parts of the country, even if that is not economic, like providing telecom facilities or laying roads or electric lines; the government is bound to provide these facilities in such far-flung areas because no private company would be interested to do that in view of no profits.

These welfare measures have helped a majority of Americans to live a better, safer, more prosperous life; while many of the problems vanished, of course, bringing other problems into existence which now needed to be tackled. Thus, forming the government is in one way like the social contract because people vote to a party which they perceive would better look after their welfare in addition to doing all those things that a government is supposed to do: administer the country well, defend it unfailingly and earn respect in the international arena. Thus, earning social respect and trust is inevitable for a government to succeed. Often, this trust cannot be maintained because the society over the centuries has become more complex, and as the President, Obama was facing it himself; he had to take into consideration more facts than an ordinary citizen would otherwise take to tackle the same problem.

Obama had come to power with a conviction that he was not there for politicking. He believed that politics should not limit itself to offer only criticism and discrimination;

he dreamed to rebuild the American people's trust, not just in the government, but outside it of it as well as well. He felt that democracy could function better if people possessed trust for one another.

Right from the earliest time Obama took over the presidentship, he was determined that the campaign promises were no more going to be mere slogans, he was going to work for them in right earnest. He meant what he had said in his election speeches. As he tried to do things, he faced a criticism that he was trying to do too much. Don't you see an analogy with what Modi had faced in his early years as the Prime Minister?

While Obama had a very busy schedule of his own, he was missing a bit of his family life, because the new post he had ushered in had also brought all his family members to play new roles. The role of the First Lady is no more limited to looking after the needs of her overly busy husband. Michelle would have been very happy if she was required to only look after her husband, maintain her persona in public, care for the family, and also be gracious with those who came or happened to meet her. Until Obama found himself in the high seat, she was following her own course of career, but it was no longer possible in the new capacity as there were complexities involved.

Despite his high stature, Obama remained an individual who felt much like other humans. He admits that he got angry during his term, especially when he found that those in power were not doing enough on matters that involved national security because they preferred their vested interests to it. He says that whenever he felt angry, he ensured that he didn't raise his voice because shouting could only worsen things and put you in bad light, while it was also equally important to express what was going in the mind.

In the East Wing of the White House, Michelle had a small suite of offices from which she ran her own errands, and had a quite busy schedule of her own. While she had a long queue of attendants to look after all their personal needs, she did not look away from her duty as the wife; she ensured that everything was comfortable for Obama as he liked. She also ensured that Malia and Sasha too were comfortable and allowed them some liberty in their childlike behaviour; and this could be seen coming into concrete when the two could be spotted bumping the balls against the corridor walls.

So far as the life in the White House was concerned, it was as normal as normal could be; but so was not the case whenever any of them needed to go out of the secure four walls.

Whenever Michelle stepped out of the White House, she sparkled with charm; and she emerged as a fashion icon. She presented herself in style, and she was seen a fit person as the First Lady, though in the initial period, she felt somewhat uncertain all about this. In this capacity, she could no more be a professional lady she once was; now millions of people, especially women looked up to her to provide the much-needed motivation, especially when the economy was in a devastating mode.

At the same time, Obama was anxious to guard her from the media glare as it often came up with unrealistic, and often contradictory, social pressures as the news reporters are often wont to pose questions on private life including children. The girls were at her heart too, and even when she was pursuing her career at the University of Chicago before she became the First Lady, she was afraid that she could deprive her daughters of quality time, and this could be true of her husband and work too, and she never wanted to do injustice to either of them. Now, it was no longer possible to keep them away from the public eye, everything had changed in the new position. She had to give up her job.

Bringing up Sasha and Malia too had undergone a vital change. The ordinary had changed into extraordinary, with a new set of complications with the head of the family in a powerful position. If Sasha needed to go on a playdate, the Secret Service agents surveyed the household to ensure that everything would be smooth. At the same time, the agents ensured that the media kept away from taking or printing pictures of the girls when they were out. Malia was in her fifth grade and Sasha was younger than her.

Obama was not merely a responsible President, and to be assessed one of the best the US have seen, he was a complete family man to the deepest core of his heart. In the South Lawn of the White House, he had got a swing set installed for Sasha and Malia, overlooking which was located his Oval Office. Even when Obama was busy in some serious business, he would steal a glance or two in the spring afternoon to see the two little girls playing outside, their faces set in bliss as they soared high on the swings. He himself took time out from his working routine to play a set of basketball or to have a quick game of H-O-R-S-E, while he encouraged his office staff to play one or the other game to keep themselves fit and motivated.

In addition to looking after the family, Michelle often went out of way to do things which earned her appreciation. To encourage healthy eating habits, she planted her own garden; it was thought to be a modest one meeting the needs of the family, but eventually it attracted worldwide attention and encouraged setting up school and community gardens in the country and abroad; at the end of the first year, the garden had started to produce much vegetable of a number of varieties, all of which could not be consumed in the White House kitchen, so crates of them were sent out to food banks across the capital. Similarly, a small beehive was set up, which led to producing almost one hundred pounds of honey a year; and a novel idea was mooted to brew it into beer, making Obama the first presidential brew master.

To keep the house active, a dog named Bo was also acquired; it was like a bundle of joy for the entire family, each of them hugging and playing with him. Michelle herself taught him tricks, and she had to listen to what the girls told her in harsh terms when she sneaked him bacon; Malia simply compared her with a bad parent. Thus, the family atmosphere in the White House was brilliant.

Michelle took up the opportunity to bring out her personality in the open in style. She now picked up several agendas like the gender discrimination, and toughest questions to her were how she looked after the girls, and she proudly called herself as 'mom in chief'. She was approached with demands for policy-making, as she was seen as the hidden force behind all government work, and such occasions were hard for her. She also started to work on childhood obesity as it was becoming a potent problem; even Sasha suffered from obesity. She found out that the so-called 'kid-friendly' foods and snacks were the real culprit and something needed to be done to keep children away from them. She also took up the cause of the soldiers, especially those serving abroad in precarious conditions in Afghanistan and Iraq.

On how should she should tackle the public perception and expectations, she also consulted Hillary Clinton and

Laura Bush, so that she could learn from their experiences, though of course, she had to form her own ways to come out the winner. Obama felt that his wife worked from the heart, and not the head; from experience rather than from abstractions. He was sure that she could chalk out her path herself.

What Michelle and girls liked best was the fact that Obama was basically home all the time, unless he was travelling outside the capital or country. Whenever he was there, he would make sure to be with his family at dinnertime, even if it meant that he needed to go back to the Oval Office after it. It was a time when they passed quality time as a family. The girls had a lot of things to talk about their life, especially about school friends and teachers; and the curious girls had a lot of questions to ask. Obama was patient with answering the little questions, because they formed the basis of a child's personality. He could not afford to neglect his aspect. He would also take joy in telling bedtime stories. He ensured that when he was in the company of the girls, they would not discuss politics, their points of interest mainly included the friends, old and new.

Talking about this quality time, Obama describes this as a 'replenishing time', because when a person was tackling so many problems of the country and world, some amount of negativity was bound to creep in, but this time helped him cleanse his inner-self. The family also accepted the staff as part of their family, whether they were chefs or gardeners or security agents or others.

Obama was already a smoker when he was sworn in; it was a vice that he had carried over from the rebel days of his youth. Like any other woman, Michelle too insisted that he quit it, and he had done it on several occasions, but he picked it back again. Of course, now he made sure that he didn't smoke before the girls or in the house. When he was elected to the Senate, he had quit smoking in public, though he never understood the rationale why he should do so. During his election campaigns, he took time to smoke during his interminable rides across the states or in his room, and he carried a pack in his drawer or suitcase all the time. Now as the president, he was virtually in public all the time, and of course at home. So, taking out time for smoking was hit hard, and then he came up with the idea. He would walk out to the pool behind the Oval Office after lunch, or climb up the third-floor terrace after Michelle and girls were fast asleep. Increased restrictions should have cut down on the cigarette intake, but it rather increased. Earlier, he had moderated to the count of four or five cigarettes a day, but now, this intake had shot up to eight, sometimes to nine or even ten. And whenever he felt content with a decision he had taken, the puff would also accompany a martini.

A person in public life has to be prudent of what he says, especially in public; an ill-thought remark could land you in trouble, and one such occasion arose when Obama called the bankers 'fat cat bankers'. He had to face the complaint when he was in a meeting with the top bankers. Obama felt that the economic crisis had a fair share of the bankers' mismanagement of the public money which they plundered on bad loans, and which devastated the economy. The bankers complained that his remarks had tarnished their images and fomented voices against them. Obama knew that he needed to control himself, so he kept his voice low but still spoke his mind saying that he was only 'standing between you and the pitchforks', meaning that he was in fact trying to guard them from public anger.

This also remains true that the head of the nation gets too much credit when things are doing well in the country, and also gets too much blame when things go wrong; though on both occasions, things might well be out of his making, or even beyond his capacity. For example, the President could be blamed for higher or lower interest rates, though they are decided by the Fed, over which he has no control. So can be the case with numerous issues, like the projects being stalled due to bad weather or natural disasters. While major presidential decisions take time to take effect, it is difficult for the President to know what impact his decision would have on the economy or other things. And the most vicious thing about all this is that the voters can well vote for or against a sitting President on issues that he could do little about. More interestingly, the President has to take decisions from the options he is presented with, and all options could be as bad as bad can be.

During his early presidentship, Obama had chalked out a strategy to deal with serious issues, and this came to be called 'stress test'. Under this, the things were allowed to open up of their own until some headway could be seen, and this also applied when some action was taken to tackle a problem, and the policy of wait and watch deemed to be the fittest. The reason for this strategy to be adopted was that not all things improved within a little time a decision was taken.

A pervasive impression in almost every American is that it is only American leadership of the world that can steer it into a better direction and bring it freedom, safety and protection; though it forgets that it is America which has enriched itself on the coffers earned through sale of arms; it can even bolster terrorists when it comes to serve its selfish interests. Even Obama was brought up with such an impression in his mind. Most of the American legislators, in states and centre, come to believe that everybody the world over depends on his or her country for protection. A country in such a state of mind cannot evade the situation when it has to face the ever-present possibility of being attacked by another power, or being drawn into a conflict in which more than one power might be involved. The Americans have been very suspicious of the Soviets and the Communists in China, and their real or perceived proxies who might want to dislodge America from its hegemonic position.

In the present global scenario, terrorist threat has become very real for most of the countries in the world, more so America, with the 9/11 being only an illustration to the gory fact that it has to invest sizeable investments and resources to ensure that it doesn't have to face any such situation ever again. Obama himself admits that he grew up with many of these fears imprinted on his psyche, and they intensified after he found his way into the state legislature, and they were at the greatest zenith when he was inaugurated as the President. Being in a superior position, an ordinary American feels how lucky s/he is to be born in that country.

In the process of asserting its superiority, inherent dangers arise for America and Americans to overcome on which they have to spend the resources which otherwise they could have spent on bettering the country, if not the world. The risk comes up from the actions which America takes in the world arena and which leaves behind a bad image in the minds of people, which could well result into anger and resentment. This remains true that it is only like a pipedream for any other power to attack the monolithic America directly, but that does not exclude the chances when some individual group or person might take chances to intrude into the zones considered safe. Such attacks have cultivated a feeling in Americans that over time, they are less safe.

Obama was always susceptible that his actions as the President might not be accepted by Americans, especially his detractors not because he could prove not so potent in the seat, but because of the fact that he came from a coloured family. He was the son of a black African with a Muslim name and socialist ideas; and when such a power was all-in-all, many Americans could feel, Obama felt, that they needed to be defended against him as well.

America has had a long history of interfering into other countries' affairs; this came to its best during the World War II, when it supplied not only munitions but also men. It was doing so even when Obama was sworn in as President. Obama felt that many people in other countries felt that their problems were mainly due to American interference, like in Indonesia. And this interference was not necessarily in military terms, it could well be in economic zone; for example, Latin Americans felt that the US companies had befouled their countryside causing widespread environmental problems. Many visitors to America felt really bad when they were pulled apart for a thorough check at the customs.

Now, for Obama, to deal with the threats, real or perceived, he could use either soft power or hard power.

His security team comprised people from both sides of the line. Many of them openly advocated for the use of brute force to bring the world situation to their favour; while others rightly understood the importance of public diplomacy and hoped to achieve a favourable world situation through aid and student-exchange programmes. Well, foreign policy is such a nasty game, we all know. It hides more than it shows.

Foreign policy for Obama involved taking decisions what role his country should play in the international organisations like the UN, and to what extent that its own interests are not compromised with. Similar is the case to deal with countries; whether it should align with authoritarian regimes to just keep a lid on the possible chaos, or go showering favours on the forces of democratic reforms. It is such a tricky business that having interaction with one country has repercussions on others too; so, a decision has to be taken that creates a favourable impact for America as a whole, without earning the ire of the international powers.

While deciding on issues involving foreign policy, Obama had to take into consideration the two divergent, often conflicting viewpoints of the two groups he had in his team. One group felt that a responsible foreign policy meant continuity, predictability and advocated that the administration should not deviate from the conventional wisdom that had been tasted earlier, for example in the form of invasion of Iraq. In contrast were those who were willing to challenge the assumptions and wanted to engage most countries diplomatically, whether they were Cuba or Iraq or Middle East. Having two types of opinions in the foreign policy didn't make things easier for him, because this could spill beans into the open. And the funniest thing with the soft power was that the Pentagon, State Department and CIA proved harder nuts to crack.

With such a situation, Obama needed to rethink the entire gamut of foreign policy afresh. He was willing to traverse in uncomfortable waters, that was to test the shortcomings the administration at his disposal had and how bad the execution of an order could result into. He decided that he should go for the customary vision and wisdom in most matters, and continue with the well-reasoned policy that had succeeded until then; after all, customs, symbols and protocols mattered much in the international relations, so did body language, much of which he had to learn under the watchful eyes of his security and foreign policy staff.

As the US President, Obama's day started with the folder called President's Daily Brief or PDB which waited for him at the breakfast table. It was prepared by the CIA overnight and contains important information that might require the President's attention. It gave him the world view and intelligence analysis that might affect the national interests, especially the war preparation and terrorist threats, even if they were unactionable, nonetheless they were included in order to keep up-to-date because the nation could no longer afford to have a recurrence of something like 9/11. After that, he proceeded to the Oval office for a briefing followed by the day-long business which might include a variety of meetings. These meetings inevitably discussed incidents of terrorism and war, as it was going on in Afghanistan and Iraq, in which a sizeable number of American troops were involved. Terrorism is a potent threat for the national economy of any country, because it involves the expenditure which otherwise could have been invested on development, alleviation of poverty and improvement of infrastructure and other vital aspects of life.

The overseas cost of the American war was dear; by Obama's early term, it had cost over a trillion dollar and three thousand dead troops with almost ten times of that wounded. The war had been started by the previous administration, but now the American psyche was turning against it, as few believed that it could result in such devastating aftermath. Even Americans were raising their voice against violation of rule of law and human rights when it came to those taken prisoners in Iraq and Afghanistan because many of them were only suspects, and they languished in Guantanamo for long terms, and often, no more of them was ever heard what became of the prisoners.

The Bush administration had already signed the broad outlines about withdrawal of troops from Iraq, and the withdrawal of combat forces was to be complete by the end of 2011. Obama wanted an earlier withdrawal, but it also involved actions so that they did not leave Iraq in a precarious situation, because the retreating forces would need to train and assist the Iraqi military. The people too approved an accelerated withdrawal. Of course, not all forces had to be taken away; a residual force had to remain there so that the country could not be thrown to chaos, especially in view of the fact that al-Qaeda had active presence and could once again strengthen after the American pull back. Obama wanted to withdraw such that he would not have to send his forces again.

However, the situation in Afghanistan was different from that of Iraq, so did Obama perceive. The Taliban there had local ambitions, but its leadership was constantly in touch with the al-Qaeda, and that could mean that a strong Taliban could spring to launch terrorist attacks in other countries, especially the US and its allies. Obama viewed Pakistan as incapable, rather unwilling, to take on terrorists taking refuge in the barely ruled region of Afghanistan-Pakistan border. It was inevitable for the US to destroy the terrorist infrastructure, and with unreliable Pakistan as an ally, he had no other option but to enter war in Afghanistan on the side of the government; thus, making it a war of necessity. This also remains true that with its rugged territory, no foreign army had ever succeeded here. Over the past six years, the situation in Afghanistan had only deteriorated only because the US had paid primary interest to Iraq. Of course, it was not totally overlooked, as about 30,000 US troops were stationed there alongside about an equal number of troops from the allies. The Taliban controlled a large area in the country along the Pakistan-Afghanistan border, and with its motivated troops, the terrorist organisation could launch effective attacks on the larger but poorly trained Afghan army. Then corruption too played its part in the government as Hamid Karzai's administration openly indulged in mismanaging international funds that were meant for uplifting the living conditions of the poor people.

The US was working in Afghanistan with two goals; one was to clear the Taliban and another was to modernise the populace. The matter became hopeless because whenever an area freed from terrorists was handed over to the local administration, they proved inefficient, leading to the terrorists once again taking over the area, thus nullifying all the gains that had been made. In view of this precarious situation, Obama instructed that his military, intelligence and civilian staff needed to work in coordination with clear goals, so that a pull-out from there could become feasible in the foreseeable future.

For now, the need to induct more troops there seemed to be the better option; and these would include trainers who would help in training the Afghan personnel for smooth election duties. There was yet another aspect to it; and that is, the military generals were always in the favour of deploying more troops, because it brings them vital resources and fulfils their ambitions; and this could not be allowed. Obama was thankfully spared the tough job as Joe Biden as his deputy had begun to ask tough questions, thus rendering the President a great service.

The truth remains, and Obama realized, that sending in troops for Iraq invasion had only broken the country leading to breeding of a more lethal form of terrorists of al-Qaeda; and now the counterinsurgency operation was costing precious lives. He did not want such things to happen with Afghanistan, because the American action in Iraq had already created a negative international attitude against the US. The step that was decided would take another five years to settle. This could not be a good deal, but other options were worse and riskier, because not inducting more troops there could mean the Afghan government collapsing and the Taliban gaining footholds in major cities; and this could be catastrophic for the world.

The idea of foreign policy is not without selfish goals, because it seeks to get facilities for the country as well as its missions and citizens abroad. It is not always meant at humiliating other countries, it is also based on mutual cooperation, and strengthening its influence. One thing was particularly kept in mind in such interactions was that the country was not merely feared, it ought to be respected as a powerful country, which would not bear with any nuisance.

The world too was changing rapidly when Obama took over the reins; the Soviet Union had already collapsed in 1991, Germany had reunified and then Europe had unified; China, though still rooted in communism looked to embrace capitalism without letting go any of its control on anything; many countries in Asia, Africa and Latin America were transitioning from authoritarian to democratic rule; apartheid had come to an end in South Africa. So many good things were happening across the globe, but that never meant that conspiracies and conflicts were going to end too.

The world was changing in economic terms too. The western world had commanded the economic scenario of the world (G-8), but then there were several large countries that had awakened from long slumbers to realize that they could turn around things and were no more satisfied with being regional powers and were willing to take the centre stage; and these nations included the BRICS (Brazil, Russia, India, China and South Africa), and these countries were well part of the G-20, playing a vital role in the world economy. The problem with these countries was, and is, that a decision in Europe or America influenced them much more than a decision that they made in their own country, and now they were embracing a situation to manifest their capability; after all, they had at their command about 40% of the global population and about a quarter of the world GDP. In wealth terms, they had many stairs to climb as yet, because they had yet to gain an important position in the World Bank and the IMF (International Monetary Fund).

Obama was willing to give more leverage to the BRICS countries as they were emerging powers, but at the same time, he insisted that they needed to take up more responsibility in the world affairs, and could not be mere beneficiaries. For the BRICS countries, he felt that these countries operated foreign policy if it served their own interests, and they followed bilateral commitments out of necessity rather than conviction, and could easily flout the agreements if their interests required so; they assisted other countries only on bilateral basis, expecting some benefit in return. He also realized that these countries were still poor though emerging, and could not afford to be charitable without having lifted out their large populations out of poverty, squalor and illiteracy.

An important point in foreign policy revolves round nuclear weapons. The world is sitting on the piles of these weapons of mass destruction which can destroy the earth several times over, yet these piles continue to enlarge and expand. Obama felt that there was an important need to start negotiations with all players in this respect so that the world could be made a safer place to live. With this in view, he started with negotiations with his Russian counterpart as a follow-up to the START (Strategic Arms Reduction Treaty); he took initiative for this during his visit to London to take part in the G-20 conference. Then there were also players that could pose a threat to world peace; Iran and Pakistan were only two of them, though he felt much confident about India's possession of these weapons.

During the course of his duty, the American President has to travel, and for this, detailed arrangements are made. He always travels in his Beast and flies in the Air Force One. When he travels abroad, the arrangements become even more detailed and elaborate, because as the most powerful nation of the world, it is insisted that glory and magnificence are manifest in every manner. His aircraft (there are two in fact) is customised Boeing 747, with heavily upholstered leather chairs, walnut tables and panelling and carpeted floor. It was complete with a built-in bedroom, private office, conference room and shower, and working desks for his team. It is unmatched in its security and safety features too with the best pilots, armoured windows and airborne refuelling capacity. Normally, his aircraft had 30 staff onboard, including pilots, Secret Service agents, medical staff and other staff from his team.

The visit of the US President is sometimes a brow-raising event for the host country, as he does not rely on any local services or security forces.

This means that before he lands in another country, an entire retinue of his security forces, Secret Service agents, Beast, security vehicles, tactical teams, ambulances are deployed to look after each minute's stay there. Not only this, even a fighting unit is stationed which is ready to take on a low-scale operation; and is backed up by the defence deployment that can undertake any operation at a very short notice. Such arrangements certainly prompt consternation from the host country, but then, all this is tolerated only because the visit of the US President is no ordinary occurrence for any country across the globe, and these arrangements are beyond any negotiation on part of the Secret Service agents.

The visit of the US President is a very important event, so people and international media become immediately interested, who try to steal a glimpse of his facilities and staff, if not he himself. Whenever he emerges from his aircraft, he stands aloft at the door and waves his hands, before climbing down. At the tarmac, he is welcomed in varied manners which might go as per the local traditions and diplomacy, and could include a guard of honour or presentation of a bouquet by a woman or child dressed in the traditional dress.

Healthcare was close to Obama's heart. To provide succour to people, he first studied the history of healthcare in the US right since the time of Theodore Roosevelt who had raised his voice for establishment of a centralised national health service, at a time when few people felt the need for private health insurance, and they paid for their treatment as and when need arose for it. Over a century, things no more remained the same as new inventions and discoveries opened newer doors of medical facilities to common people leading to costly treatment; and this was the reason that the need for a national health insurance scheme became the necessity for the nation, much on the line of several other countries including UK.

In the past century, people's vision to affordable and accessible medical treatment changed to viewing it as a right and not mere privilege. The Second World War brought in further changes when the companies provided private medical insurance and other facilities to the workers; and this arrangement continued in the times to come.

This of course had a negative impact on the government which did not like to take initiative to provide this facility to common people, and further momentum to this thinking was provided by private players who described the government's intervention in this field as 'socialised medicine'. In the fifties, the government targeted those people who could not afford modern medicine, and this laid the path for all of the people viewing it as a right. As we can see in India today, an illness could mean the family's financial ruin, so was the case there in the middle of the century, because a sizeable number of redundant tests and overcharging for drugs was the norm, making the US medical expenditure per person the costliest in the western world.

When Obama took over, he saw that both insured and uninsured people were suffering; the former on account of the rising insurance costs and the latter for paying for the expensive drugs and tests. Due to high costs of treatment, the uninsured people waited until they were quite sick to access medical facilities, as they knew it was going to ruin them. While a large number of people had insurance, people, in general, were not much interested in the government interfering in this segment. However, the new President felt otherwise, though his advisers thought that an earlier effort in this direction in 2004 had led to Democrats' losing majority in the Senate, and this could be the same this time around too. He, however, felt that there was need to provide succour to common people and rally them behind his initiative for their betterment, and this could not be done without taking an extensive step because the stakeholders could try to spoil the game. It was no political or policy matter for him; it came from his heart. So, the first need was to form public opinion in his favour.

With creation of a positive atmosphere in the country, now was the turn of legislative process to take root, and that was not going to be easy either. In politics, your opponents never want you to take credit for anything great that might happen, and take responsibility for all that bad happens. The healthcare bill moved ahead when the House committees passed it in some basic form in 2009, and now the different versions of the bill had to be consolidated into the final shape, and then would require the monumental effort to bring in all the vested interests to support it.

The result was positive; the bill was finally passed in the Senate with 216 votes in favour. This was how the American healthcare system was to come into existence which would eventually be popularly called Obamacare.

Good work led to the announcement of the Nobel Peace Prize in October 2009, though he was yet to complete even one year in office. He expressed to the press that he didn't feel himself deserving it because he didn't see himself as a transformative figure, like those who had been conferred the high award in the past; rather he saw it as a call to action so that he could work better to reduce the threat of nuclear weapons and work for issues pertaining to climate change that could threaten the very humanity. Personally, he was of the opinion that the US needed to cut down its emissions to help in the cause of climate change. He also spoke of many other issues that could make the world a better place to live; and these included equality of human rights and uplift of living, eradication of conflict of all kinds. As if this was not a big enough news, another one, a tragic one, poured from Afghanistan in which the Afghan militants had overrun a US military outpost killing eight and wounding twenty-seven more. Terrorism was growing so menacing, and concrete steps needed to be taken in right earnest.

When it came to deal with terrorists, Obama was sombre, ruthless, though feeling mercy at the same time for the person to be targeted at. Early on his presidency, he had to order the killing of a group of Somali pirates who had taken hostage of an American captain Phillips from the ship Maersk Alabama. He felt pity for these pirates and terrorists because they were all very young who often did not understand things how they had been misguided, and they should have been holding books and laptops instead of guns. He felt that they had been warped and stunted by desperation and ignorance; they had been misguided by claims of religious glory by the so-called religious people. Their teachings had made them ruthless and cruel.

Despite his pity, Obama was forced to give orders to end their lives. Whenever he gave such orders, he felt restless. To execute such orders, the American forces had acquired infrastructure, installed it at places where it was needed most, like in Pakistan and Afghanistan, and had trained hard to overcome any such threats, and had devised new forms of intelligence gathering and analysis of the acquired information. On the whole, it was a tricky task. At the same time, he started humanitarian efforts so that some relief to the prisoners accused of terrorism could be brought; and one such step was the closing down of the Gitmo, the military prison at Guantanamo

Bay, where the inmates were detained for indefinite periods without any trial; this meant that the detainees would have access to the legal system. He also appointed doctors to look after the sick or wounded terrorists; thus, Obama's pity was becoming manifest in actions too. This helped to bring down the number of prisoners there by about 5% in two years.

From the time of Bush administration, a practice to announce 'Top 20' terrorists had been adopted. This list comprised all vital information about the terrorist complete with photographs; and whenever any kill from the list was made, another target was added to it so the list had to contain 20 names; and instructions to eliminate them were clear; so the forces were perennially engaged in locating these culprits who had brought the world to its toes depriving the vital funds which otherwise could have been invested for better causes to bring relief to the suffering masses the world over.

Despite the resources at his command, Obama took no joy in ordering these killings, nor did he feel powerful by it. Despite this personal feeling, he had to ensure that all the operations had to be effective and to-the-point. Ultimately, dealing with a ruthless enemy, one has to become ruthless himself else he would be given a lever to conflict harm upon oneself. The worst thing about terrorists was (and is) that they thwart their own designs and agreements at the slightest plea; still they try to show them as victims; and ingraining this feeling in the youth has enabled them to recruit more and more terrorists.

The terrible thing about counterterrorism operations for the US was that these did not involve only aerial bombing or targeting from distance; the troops had to be physically present in the war theatre often fighting hand-to-hand battles, and suffering casualties. When wounded or dead soldiers started to land in the mainland America, people came to know the worse consequences of the country's participation in other countries' affairs in the name of national security. Obama had opposed this decision when Bush took this decision; but now he himself was in the high seat, yet was unable to take recourse to pull out; the job had to be finished so that the sacrifices made by the soldiers and taxpayers did not go in vain.

Obama, however, was of the opinion that they needed to reform their counterterrorism practices so as to minimise risks and damage; and he gave instructions for replacing the existing warfare and intelligence practices with better ones, but he realized that it had to be a slow and grinding exercise. The steps like closing down of the Gitmo could not go without adverse consequences in the international arena because legal processes would require declassifying documents and photographs which could put the American forces in a very bad light. Transparency in operations could also mean putting the counterterrorist operations in jeopardy; so much more thinking had to be made part of the entire process.

He also decided to go onboard with two speeches in which he could deal with the issue of terrorism and antagonism that had occurred between the western world and the Muslim world. In the first, he spoke on the need for long-term national security goals to be depended on fidelity to the Constitution and the rule of law, acknowledging that, following the 9/11, the country had fallen short of these ideals, and how he now sought to rebuild relations.

The second speech he was to deliver in Cairo and focussed on the relation between the two worlds. He knew that the attitudes in these (Muslim) countries could not be changed overnight, yet there was need to start the process so that the goal of peaceful coexistence could be set, else the wars would remain on the horizon for a few more decades to come, bringing only avoidable misery and destruction. The second speech was trickier in sense because America had been depicted in the Muslim world as antagonistic to Muslims and Islam; but its focus was geared towards building understanding between the two worlds.

His speech in Cairo was well received by people, clerics and leaders; though it was a bare fact that any one speech could not change the Middle East; it had to be supported by a long-term action on part of the western and Muslim worlds. Even a positive action has its fallout, so was the case with Obama's Cairo speech. It had raised expectations, but that was doomed to disappoint them; there is too much gap between the ground realities and ideal conditions to be bridged.

Obama felt a great kinship with the families of those killed in counterterrorism operations in Afghanistan and Iraq, and he himself sent the letters to the kin of the brave-hearts in the middle of the terrible war. He has said in his autobiography that he signed these letters very slowly ensuring that there was no smudge and the letter was signed as to leave an emotional impression on the reader. In case he was not satisfied with his signature on any letter, he would get it reprinted. He was not the only one in the White House to correspond with the families.

Those in public office the world over have to face situations that are beyond their control because they cannot push it under the carpet; only time becomes the biggest healer. There are rough patches that a politician goes through, and these may arise out of some mistake, or some unforeseen circumstance, or the failure to communicate in time, and the press thinks it should be brought out louder; the media bash goes on unabated until the problem has been fixed or something more important comes to happen which deviates the media and people attention to it. In case the problem persists longer, it may bring the politician in bad light.

Obama too had to face this situation several times over during his term at the supreme post, but he ensured that he tackled all of them timely so that it did not blow up beyond control, but then you know it is not at all possible, especially when the opponents are working to bring you and your prestige down. To douse a fire, Obama needed to immediately explain the actual situation so that people didn't panic in case of a terrorist or other terrible occurrence, but sometimes it took longer for him as it could not be feasible for him to speak his opinion without all the facts at his table, and garnering all the facts often took more time than thought.

Carrying out military strikes deep inside another country is no simple task; it draws a lot of international attention and nations can be taking varying stands. So far as America is concerned, it has been doing so for decades; Syria, Libya, Iraq and Afghanistan are only a few to name. However, when the President needs to order such strikes inside a country that has been known to be a longstanding ally, it could involve a lot of complications. In 2011, when Obama needed to tread a precautionary route to re-election a few months later, he was faced with an issue that had all the potential of making or marring his chances to remain in the high office; and it was none else but Osama bin Laden. The intelligence agencies had zeroed in on a target that they believed to be the dreaded terrorist stationed deep inside Pakistan. If he got it right, there was little that could obstruct his path to re-election, else his chances were doomed. In such a tricky situation, he was to decide whether to take action or just to give it a shrug; after all, all targets cannot be hit, and many of them can misfire.

Laden was a creation of the US whims, and had earned a bad reputation with the US authorities following

9/11 in which over innocent 3,000 people had been killed when terrorists crashed aeroplanes into high-rises. Ever since, he was being searched, and when his location was sighted at Tora Bara, a mountainous area along Afghan-Pak border, the US-led allies closed in, but he escaped, and ever since not much was known about his whereabouts.

And now there was a lead that he could be in Pakistan; the most pertinent question was whether the lead was right or not. As for Obama, he had criticised the US forces being sent to Iraq; but now, there was a sizeable US force abroad fighting wars and suffering sizeable casualties, and this had put the country on a greater risk as it was being viewed as the greatest enemy of the Muslims and Islam.

Laden was in hiding, nonetheless he remained the most effective recruiter of jihadis who were motivated through his video and audio messages. His being alive and working was like mocking at the mighty US. The intelligence agencies had been on the lookout for Laden, but he was like an ass's horns, visible nowhere.

And now after a long time, leads had traced an al-Qaeda courier having close ties with Laden. Extensive surveillance of the man led them to a large compound on the outskirts of Abbottabad in Pakistan, quite close to the capital Islamabad. This massive compound, surrounded by high walls, pointed that somebody important lived there, and more importantly, the inhabitants lived in total secrecy, without a landline or internet service, but the question lingered if he was Laden. There were more facts which pointed to something fishy; for example, the inhabitants never left the premises and their trash was burned and not disposed outside the premises. The number and age of children matched to those of Laden's family members. Aerial observation also found a tall man who walked around the compound; and this man could, in all probability, be Laden. If any more efforts were made to ascertain his identity, he could vanish again, so this risk could not be taken.

Obama was convinced with the inference and made up his mind that a raid could be made, but then there were other problems. Pakistan was an ally, still it could not be believed as its military and intelligence service (ISI) had deep links with terrorists including the Taliban and possibly al-Qaeda, so the raid had to be conducted in complete secrecy. But then raid meant a reprehensive act of violation of its sovereignty, the act by itself could be deemed an act just short of war. It was also sure that Pakistan's army could not oppose, but then ties were sure to sore. There was also an option to conduct a missile attack, but in that case, it would never be known if it was really Laden. Moreover, it could also mean a violent death to women and children. So, a raid seemed to be the only viable answer, but it was risky.

The raid had to be a completely covert operation, in which the commandoes would fly into Pakistan by helicopter, and finish the job before the Pakistani military or police had time to react. Of the two main agencies that could carry out the operation - CIA and Navy SEAL, the latter was chosen because of its skill and experience in similar operations.

For Obama, the main concern was whether the raid could be executed successfully, and two weeks' practice led them to believe that it could be. It was planned that the commandoes would fly in from Jalalabad in Afghanistan under the cover of darkness on a moonless night, secure all entry points of the compound, and then search the three-storey building, neutralising any resistance that could arise, and kill or arrest Laden.

Yet another aspect was that the helicopters could be intercepted by Pakistani aircraft while going to or out of Abbottabad. There was also a probability that searching out Laden in the building could prove tricky and consume more time than expected, and in the meantime the Pakistani forces could surround the compound. The strategy for this situation was not to engage in a firefight, and then let US diplomats take over to negotiate the return of the commandoes, but then it could not be an easy job especially in view of the Pakistani people opposing any American intrusion into its territory, which had happened in previous cases too, and things could prove very precarious in case the tall man was not Laden.

While the final decision was pending, the duly trained SEAL team and assault helicopters had been flown to Jalalabad, awaiting final orders. And finally, the decision was made. Most advisors recommended the raid, despite all probability of things going awry, and Obama gave the final call. The plan also included the actions that needed to be taken about the outcome, including establishment of communication with the Pakistani authorities and also burial of Laden at sea, so that his grave or tomb did not turn out to be a pilgrimage site for the terrorists. There was no point in postponing the decision because no new leads were coming up, and there was every possibility that the plan could leak.

And finally, the D-day arrived. Obama was all along either in the Situation Room or in constant touch with it, and when the helicopters took off with 23 SEAL commandoes together with a translator and a military dog named Cairo. He sat with his team to watch as the Operation Neptune's Spear started to unfold before his eyes. The Situation Room was in direct contact with the team, which flew for one hour and a half to reach its target in Abbottabad.

When the team approached the compound, Obama shifted to the nearby room, where Brigadier General Brad Webb was watching the proceedings on a computer screen. As Obama entered, he tried to give his seat to Obama, but the President asked him to sit down and found a place to sit in the adjacent chair. He had left the

Situation Room so that his team did not get the impression he was actually leading a military operation; the credit should go to those who deserved.

It was like a shock to everybody when a helicopter lurched and brushed against the side wall of the compound. Will it crash? The pertinent question loomed large, pushing Obama to the edge of the seat. He was assured that the pilot was the best and he would safely land the aircraft, and this was what actually happened.

The commandoes immediately got into action, searching the premises; only shadows appeared on the screen in the darkness, and then sounded the words which Obama was waiting to hear: Geronimo IDd (enemy identified) and Geronimo EKIA (enemy killed in action). Geronimo was the codename for Laden. The most dreaded terrorist had been brought to justice, what he deserved best.

Now, the SEAL team was finishing its task; it bagged Laden's body, secured three women and nine children present there and questioned them, collected all possible evidence that could be collected including computers, files, papers and whatever else that seemed of intelligence value. Before the team mounted the one still operational helicopter, another Chinook helicopter had arrived there to help in rescue of the team, and the damaged helicopter was attached with explosives, so that little evidence was left behind. The helicopters took off to safety, while the Situation Room came alive with shouts and whistles; each congratulating the other; though tension prevailed until the helicopters finally and safely landed at Jalalabad.

In the end, only formalities were left to be completed. The body was recognised through facial recognition software and it confirmed his identity; still the DNA was conducted whose results could take one or two days to come.

The Pakistani army chief was conveyed that an American military helicopter had crashed in Abbottabad, giving him jitters. The US diplomats were now getting in touch with foreign governments and press, while Obama was bracing himself with the words that he could express before the media. Obama has written that the Pakistani President Asif Ali Zardari welcomed the news and expressed support. Obama felt relieved while the world was abuzz with the news that Laden had been neutralised; celebration was in the air everywhere. Many wanted to see the photo of the dead Laden, but Obama felt otherwise; he did not want to give the jihadists a rallying point.

When Obama met the SEAL unit that had carried out the raid, no one told him in briefing who of them had fired at Laden, nor did he ask; it was a team work and everybody deserved kudos right from the pilots to the commandoes to the translator who stood guard shooing away any onlookers.

❑❑

Laurels and Later

Obama is considered one of the most highly admired presidents of the US. He had electrified his office with his landmark decisions and had deep impression on a number of national, economic and social aspects of the country. In the first two years, he accomplished a sterling performance when he took bold decisions in different aspects of national life. He continued with these achievements throughout the remaining term of his presidency. During this period, he signed a number of landmark bills into law, some of which we have discussed in the foregoing pages. The most important ones of these have been the Affordable Care Act (better known as Obamacare), the Dodd-Frank Wall Street Reform and Consumer Protection Act, and the Don't

Ask, Don't Tell Repeal Act of 2010, the American Recovery and Reinvestment Act of 2009 and the Tax Relief, Unemployment Insurance Reauthorisation, and Job Creation Act of 2010. Through all these, he tackled the Great Recession that he had inherited. To further reform economy, he brought in budget controls, and gave further impetus to economy in several ways. He also worked for wage renewal and increase so as to bridge the gap between income inequalities.

Obama worked over time to regulate greenhouse gases, and proposed new rules and regulations for power plants, factories and oil refineries in an attempt to limit greenhouse gas emissions and to curb global warming. When an explosion occurred in an offshore drilling rig in the Gulf of Mexico, he himself visited the site

He was in favour of reducing international tensions, so he ordered increase in US troops levels in Afghanistan, entered the New START treaty with Russia to reduce the number of nuclear warheads, and ended military involvement in Iraq. He contributed to forces in Libya for implementation of the UN Security Council Resolution 1973 which led to the overthrow of Muammar Gaddafi. The most spectacular of the surgical strikes ordered by him included those which led to elimination of Osama bin Laden and Anwar al-Awlaki, and several other important operatives of different terrorist organisations around the world.

Obama was sworn in for the second term in 2013. During this period, he worked for people's rights including LGBT and same-sex marriage rights, leading to their legalisation in 2015. He worked for gun control as it was leading to a menacing atmosphere in the country. He also worked to take actions on global warming and immigration.

He was bold in taking decisions, like imposing sanctions on Russia against its invasion of Ukraine and its perceived interference in the US elections. He also worked for better ties with Iran, Cuba and Israel with an intention to leave behind a better world. He took several foreign policy initiatives in several countries, which also include the famed nuclear deal with Manmohan Singh government in India. He travelled widely across the globe, and proved himself a world leader in right sense of the word.

Obama's two terms in office finally ended in 2017, when Donald Trump replaced him. Now, he continues to reside in Washington DC. The same year in March, he was awarded the Profile in Courage Award for his enduring commitment to democratic ideals and elevating the standard of political courage. Presently, he passes his time doing social service and writing books. He has a number of popular books to his credit, including the latest one *A Promised Land*, which was on a reported $65 million deal with the Penguin Random House.

Obama does not shy away from expressing his views. After Trump announced his decision to withdraw from the Paris Agreement, he was quick to point out in his prolific style: "But even in the absence of American leadership, even as this administration joins a small handful of nations that reject the future; I'm confident that our states, cities, and businesses will step up and do even more to lead the way, and help protect for future generations the one planet we've got". Again, when the bill for Better Care Reconciliation Act of 2017 was being drafted by the next administration, he categorically said that it was 'a bill that will raise costs, reduce coverage, and roll back protections for older Americans and people with pre-existing conditions'. He also criticised Trump's failure to contain the Covid pandemic, calling it 'an absolute chaotic disaster'.

He keeps raising his concerns on matters especially concerning national security, climate change and healthcare; he had worked devotedly in these three spheres in particular, and he does not want the advantage to disappear by any gimmicks.

In the capacity of a private citizen now, Obama makes international visits; he had made one such visit to India in December 2017, when he met Prime Minister Narendra Modi and also spoke at the Hindustan Times Leadership summit. He also met Dalai Lama here and also held a town hall for young leaders on the aegis of the Obama Foundation.

Obama and Michelle signed a deal in 2018 to produce docu-series, documentaries and features for Netflix under the newly established production company named Higher Ground Productions. Its first film, American Factory won the Academy Award for Best Documentary Feature in 2020.

Due to his monumental work against terrorism, he is subjected to terrorist threats. A package, addressed to him, containing a pipe bomb was intercepted by the Secret Service in October 2018. In 2020, he endorsed Joe Biden, his former vice president, who ultimately became the President in 2021.

At the time of his demitting office in 2017, he was assessed with a 60% approval rating, and the historians ranked him the 8th-Greatest American President, by all means a great record when he was put along with great American presidents of the like of Lincoln and George Washington.

He is a great leader and continues to be a popular personality the world over.